Celebration

A Play

Keith Waterhouse and Willis Hall

A SAMUEL FRENCH ACTING EDITION

SAMUEL FRENCH

FOUNDED 1830

SAMUELFRENCH-LONDON.CO.UK
SAMUELFRENCH.COM

Celebration

These plays were first presented at the Playhouse Theatre, Nottingham, and subsequently at the Duchess Theatre, London, on 7th June 1961. In the London production the cast was as follows:

I. THE WEDDING

The Bride

CHRISTINE LUCAS	*Carole Mowlam*

The Bride's Family

RHODA LUCAS (HER MOTHER)	*Gabrielle Hamilton*
EDGAR LUCAS (HER FATHER)	*James Cossins*
JACK LUCAS (HER BROTHER)	*Colin George*
IRENE HOWES (HER COUSIN)	*Virginia Stride*
LILIAN HOWES (HER AUNT)	*Hilary Hardiman*
FRANK BROADBENT (HER UNCLE)	*Jeremy Kemp*
ARTHUR BROADBENT (HER GREAT-UNCLE)	*Morgan Sheppard*
STAN DYSON (IRENE'S FIANCÉ)	*Donald Burton*

The Groom

BERNARD FULLER .. .. '.. ..	*Michael Williams*

The Groom's Family

EDNA FULLER (HIS MOTHER)	*Thelma Barlow*
ALICE FULLER (HIS AUNT)	*Gillian Martell*
LIONEL FULLER (HIS COUSIN)	*Antony Tuckey*
MARGO FULLER (HIS COUSIN'S WIFE)	*Rowena Cooper*

Directed by VAL MAY: *décor by* GRAHAM BARLOW

No character, in this play, is intended to portray any specific person, alive or dead.

PRODUCTION NOTE

CELEBRATION is written in two parts: THE WEDDING and THE FUNERAL —and both parts are complete in themselves. However, although both acts of this play can be performed singly as one-act plays it is essential that, when produced together, they be considered as a whole and not approached in direction with the technique used when handling a double bill. Probably the most rewarding factor in a production of this play will be the team-work involved, for the play is written without starring parts and as a study in family relationships for sixteen actors and actresses of approximately equal talents. Much of the success of the West End production of CELEBRATION was due to the fact that the whole of the Nottingham Playhouse Company was transported intact to London—and the play was performed by a group of players who had been working together for many months, and therefore worked as a team reliant upon overall achievement rather than individual performance.

CELEBRATION is, essentially, a group play in which every character is equally important and the director will find it helpful if, as a starting point, he studies the structure of the two main families involved—the Lucases and the Fullers—before he begins to build up single characterizations. Also it is necessary that the weight of the play be shared evenly by all the cast: if, for example, too much stress is laid on the bride and groom in the first act, the second half of the production will be thrown off-balance. It is also very important that the friction between the two families—the bickerings and arguments—be brought out and, with this in mind, a great deal will depend on careful grouping, particularly in the case of THE WEDDING. There will be little or no development in a production where two members of the cast are seen arguing in one scene and then, in the next, observed arranging the decorations together.

A word about accents. Although the play is set in the north of England the director should not attempt to build up a false and dated world of cloth caps, mufflers and "eeh bah gum" asides. The characters contained in this play are the people of today—they may live in slum houses and meet in street-corner pubs, but within a month or two they might equally be living in neat semi-detached houses on a well-planned council estate and spending their Saturday evenings in a slick, modern-fronted roadhouse-type inn. They all prefer a night round the telly to an afternoon round the public bandstand. The director should stamp out immediately any attempts by his cast to talk about t'cake or t'funeral, etc.—a north country accent is not acquired, as is widely held, simply by dropping the definite article. Similarly, it would be detrimental to the play for characters to slip into their dialogue comic north country kitchen comedy colloquialisms in an attempt to conquer the idiom—it will do nothing of the kind. If a member of the cast has difficulty with the accent it will be better to leave it well alone and concentrate solely on speech rhythms.

A short note about the humorous content of the play: although many of the lines are intentionally funny they are all naturalistic and, in playing, the humour will only be fully realized if they are played realistically. The slightest attempt to "play for laughs" even in the smallest degree, will only mar the production. Realism should be the first aim and, if this is attained, the comedy will take care of itself.

CELEBRATION is a simple, straightforward play—essentially about simple and straightforward people. The main problem in production is likely to be that of the director's in handling the large cast, most of whom are on stage throughout—particularly in THE WEDDING where the majority of the cast are not only present during much of the act but are also engaged in background activity. The level at which this activity is to take place should be carefully considered by the director before the rehearsals are begun. It will, of course, be obvious that the physical preparations should never obtrude on the dialogue and actions in the script. However, the feeling that something is being done should always be present during THE WEDDING and, occasionally, it would add to this feeling if unimportant lines of the dialogue were lost under the activity—or delivered from the rear of the stage while preparations were going on centre-front.

The characters themselves should not present any great difficulty but, for the benefit of the cast, here is a brief note on each one which might prove useful in providing a starting point from which to "set" the interpretation.

CHRISTINE	Twenty-three years old. An ordinary pleasant girl.
RHODA	Middle-aged, a plump and pleasant woman.
EDGAR	Also middle-aged, balding and of a rather retiring nature.
JACK	Twenty-six. Single, bombastic nature.
IRENE	Nineteen. A plain, slow girl with an obviously low I.Q.
LILIAN	Irene's mother. A small, thin-lipped woman.
FRANK	In his mid-forties. The most prosperous member of the family and very conscious of this fact.
ARTHUR	About sixty. He is more or less permanently, though not too obviously, drunk.

STAN	Nineteen years old, an aggressive, wiry young man.
BERNARD	Twenty-five. An ordinary pleasant young man lacking in personality.
EDNA	A wisp of a woman, perpetually concerned about her health who continually scratches the backs of her hands.
ALICE	A fat, breathless, middle-aged woman.
LIONEL	In his mid-twenties. Polite, and in this company, almost unctuous. A high-pitched voice.
MARGO	In her early twenties. A cheerful slut who shuffles about in old slippers.
MAY	In her fifties. A blowsy, badly made-up woman with ginger hair.
TOMMY	In his forties. A small and sprightly man who makes more use of the army than the army makes of him.

Neither of the settings should provide any problem and, of course, naturalism should be the keynote in both. A suggestion for THE WEDDING is that the set be dressed with cigarette ends, empty pint glasses, beer bottles, etc., in order to suggest that a meeting of some kind has taken place in the room the previous evening. This will not only help to provide a stale and uninviting atmosphere to the room, but will also aid the director in providing business in the way of clearing up the room—also it will help in pointing the eventual transformation at the fall of the curtain. In the case of smaller societies wishing to economize on detail the action in THE FUNERAL could be set entirely in the living-room, the hall being dispensed with by setting a door leading directly to the street and another leading to the cellars; this would necessitate only minor alterations to the text.

KEITH WATERHOUSE
WILLIS HALL

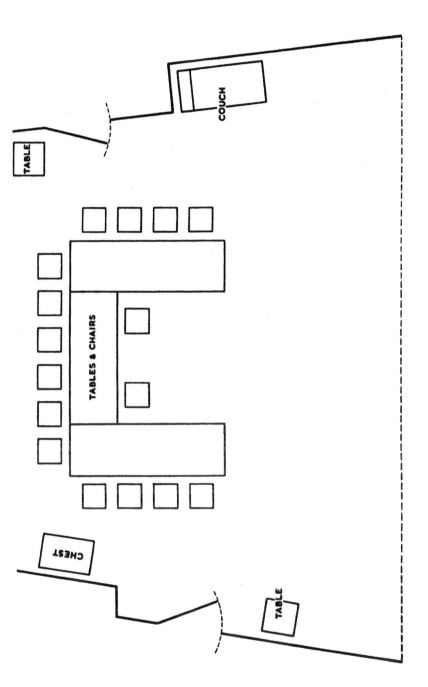

THE WEDDING

The play is set in a large and rather dingy room above the "Cricketers Arms"—a public house in an industrial town in the north of England. The room, which is on the first floor, is rarely used except when it is hired out for "social functions". It contains nothing in the way of furniture except for some rickety trestle-tables and chairs.

As the curtain rises we discover RHODA *and* EDGAR LUCAS, *a middle-aged couple, and their son* JACK, *busily preparing the room for the next day's festivities. It has been taken over by the* LUCAS *family for their daughter's wedding reception.* RHODA *is unpacking cups, plates, etc., from a tea-chest and* EDGAR *and* JACK *are wrestling with the intricacies of the trestle-tables.* EDGAR *is having difficulty with one of the tables. He rises in disgust.*

EDGAR. You should have got Whittaker's. We wouldn't have had all this palaver then.

RHODA. Oh, shut up about Whittaker's.

EDGAR. Well, you wouldn't listen, would you? We could have got a quotation. They do everything. They come in the night before and put the tables up, they come in on the morning and fetch the cake and put all the decorations up and they have two women to wait on. You don't have all this messing about with them.

(JACK *crosses and struggles with the table that has defeated* EDGAR.)

RHODA. You just get on with what you're doing. I've been to some of Whittaker's do's. You get a scuttering bit of lettuce—a tomato, and a jelly and it's all paper plates with them. You don't want paper plates when somebody's getting married.

EDGAR. No, and we don't want the blooming table to collapse when we're half-way through—'cause that's what this one's going to do.

(JACK *has, by now, fixed the table and is placing it on its feet.*)

JACK. It's all right. What are you talking about?

EDGAR. It's all right now, but it won't be all right tomorrow.

JACK. It's all right, I say. It's done. It's finished.

EDGAR. It might look all right—to you. I've put these things up before. There's that little hook missing. Three or four pork pies on that and the whole lot'll go for a burton.

JACK (*thumping the table*). There you are! What's wrong with that? There's nought wrong with that.

EDGAR. Just sit on it. Go on! You're the one that's saying it's all right. Just try sitting on it.

JACK. What are you talking about? There won't be nobody sitting on it. They'll be sitting on chairs.

EDGAR. If it was anything to do with our Christine they wouldn't have anything to sit on. What does she reckon she's doing any road?

RHODA. There's hundred and one things she's got to do. She's had her shoes to get; she's had to go down to work to collect her cards and her present and she's got that pink underslip to get shortened to go away in.

EDGAR. She wants to get married before she starts worrying about pink underslips.

RHODA. Well, she can't do everything herself. It's an honour for you, is this. You don't seem to appreciate that.

JACK. It's not an honour for me. We could have been playing darts tonight.

RHODA. I wonder you don't wear a dart-board round your neck, 'cause it's about all you've got time for. You're always "darting" it. Our Christine's getting married tomorrow, if you did but know it.

EDGAR (*wrestling to secure the last trestle-table he glances up*). We should have got Whittaker's then we wouldn't have had all this bother.

RHODA. Well, we didn't get Whittaker's so that's all there is to it.

(EDGAR *starts to put on his coat.*)

What's up with you? Are you cold?

EDGAR. I've finished.

RHODA. What do you mean, you've finished? What do you think they're going to eat off?

JACK (*putting on his coat*). Tables.

RHODA. We know they're going to eat off tables. But not like that. What do you think cloths are for? They all want covering, them tables do yet.

EDGAR. We haven't got any cloths. That's what I've been saying. If you'd got Whittaker's they'd have brought cloths with them.

RHODA. I'll cloth you if you don't shut up about Whittaker's. We've got these rolls of grease-proof paper they sent us.

EDGAR. On the cheap! On the cheap! Eating your wedding reception off grease-proof paper!

RHODA (*pulling out some rolls of grease-proof paper from a crate and tossing them to* EDGAR). You've got your drawing-pins—you just get on with it.

(RHODA *returns to unpacking the crockery as* EDGAR *and* JACK *remove their jackets.*)

EDGAR. I've never heard of grease-proof paper at a wedding before.

JACK. You haven't lived.

(EDGAR *takes a packet of drawing-pins from his pocket and, together with* JACK, *begins to tack the paper along the trestle-tables.*)

EDGAR. Where's he think he is, anyway.

JACK. Who?

EDGAR. The happy bridegroom—Donald Duck. Who do you think?

JACK. I don't know. How do I know? I don't know where he is.

EDGAR (*calling across to* RHODA). I say, where is he then? Bernard?

RHODA. I don't know where he is. He'll be out with his pals, I suppose. Buying them a drink.

JACK. That'll be the day! That'll be a famous day in history. The day he puts his hand in his pocket.

RHODA. He'll be out with his mates. Got to have his night out before he gets married. And you want those drawing-pins under the table where they don't show—not on top of it.

(EDGAR *and* JACK *return to their task as the door opens and* IRENE HOWES, EDGAR's *niece, enters.* IRENE *is carrying a tray of cutlery.*)

IRENE. I didn't know what knives to fetch, Auntie Rhoda, so I fetched them all.

(JACK, *although fond of* IRENE, *is inclined to be ruthless in his attitude towards her simplicity.*)

JACK. She's come. She's here, she's made it. Didn't you get lost, love?

IRENE. No. I've been here before. Have I to put these knives down, Auntie Rhoda?

RHODA (*patiently*). Put them on that table over there, love. Not on them cups.

(IRENE *crosses obediently and places the tray on the indicated table.*)

IRENE. No, 'cause we couldn't make out which knives you wanted. So my Mam said, "Well, you'd better be on the safe side and take them all—then you won't be blamed for it."

RHODA (*showing the first sign of dissent*). What's she want to talk like that for. Why should I blame you? We know you do your best.

EDGAR. Well, you know what she means. She doesn't mean you'll blame her—she just wanted to do right.

RHODA. I know very well what she means.

(IRENE *crosses and interestedly watches* EDGAR *and* JACK *at work.* JACK, *seeing the girl watching him, begins to tease her.*)

JACK. Did you bring me that ten bob down?

IRENE. What ten bob?

JACK. That ten bob. Didn't my Uncle Willie give you one?

IRENE. No.

JACK. Well, that puts me right in it, that does then. Are you sure you haven't lost it?

IRENE. He never gave me one.

JACK. We're lost without that ten bob note. We were banking on it. How do you think we're going to pay for this lot?

(*It dawns upon* IRENE *that she is being teased.*)

IRENE. You need more than ten bob to pay for all this, I know.

(RHODA *calls across the room to* JACK.)

RHODA. I've told you before—stop mocking her. Take no notice of him, love. You come over here and wipe these cups for me.

(IRENE *crosses to help* RHODA.)

JACK (*to* EDGAR). She takes it all in, you know. She believes everything you tell her. I laugh.

EDGAR. You just want to look what you're doing. You're putting them drawing-pins all wrong.

(IRENE *and* RHODA *are now wiping the cups and saucers with tea-towels.*)

RHODA. It's no use just doing the outside—'cause we don't know where they've been, these cups. They send them out all over.

IRENE. It's best to use your own. But there's too many, isn't there? You wouldn't have enough to go round, would you?

RHODA. No, love.

IRENE. When Alice Logan got married she had them paper cups—paper plates and that. I don't like them. I think they look common (*She thinks.*) It saves you washing up though.

RHODA. It makes it all taste. Did your mother say anything? About what time she was coming round?

IRENE. No. She was just waiting in for the insurance man.

RHODA. Well, did she say what time she would be coming?

IRENE. She said she didn't know whether to come down or not. She said she didn't know whether she'd be wanted.

RHODA. How does she mean, she wouldn't be wanted?

IRENE. She said: "You'd better take them all down, them knives. You'd better be on the safe side." She says, "If anybody gets the blame it won't be you."

EDGAR (*approaching* RHODA). I hope you realize it's too narrow—this grease-proof paper.

RHODA. Oh, stop putting difficulties in my way.

EDGAR. It's all right you saying difficulties. You know what your Frank's like. He's not used to sitting down to grease-proof paper. He doesn't sit down to grease-proof paper where he goes. He's used to being waited on—hand and foot.

RHODA. Our Frank doesn't care. He's not proud.

EDGAR. It doesn't matter whether he's proud or not. He'll expect more than a bit of jelly and a tongue sandwich. It's what he's got accustomed to.

IRENE. Me Mam says she was surprised you didn't go to Whittaker's.

RHODA (*sharply*). Well, your Mam hasn't got it to pay for, has she?

IRENE. No, but she knows him. Mr. Whittaker. She says he's very good.

JACK (*approaching the group*). Hey, where did you get these drawing-pins from? 'Cause you want to take them back. They keep breaking.

RHODA (*impatiently*). Oh, get on with you—drawing-pins! Just get on with what you've got to do!

EDGAR. It's all right you saying—there's more than drawing-pins to think about. It tears does that paper. You've only to spill a jug of tea on it and it's had it. It's not even proper grease-proofed. Cheap! On the cheap!

IRENE. My Mam wanted to know if you wanted to borrow a couple of bed sheets. She thought you'd be having more table-cloths.

RHODA (*more sharply*). Tell her thank you very much, but we've got fixed up.

EDGAR. What are you getting at her for? She's only trying to help.

RHODA. It's not her—it's your Lilian. She's forever finding fault.

EDGAR. She's been a good friend to you when you've needed her. Who did all our cooking and cleaning that time you were in hospital?

RHODA. Yes, we know all about that. I came back home and there was cups thick with grease. And what did she want to put dripping in that Coronation mug for?

EDGAR. Well, she didn't know where you kept your dripping.

RHODA. No, and she didn't look either. And you didn't have the sense to tell her—you were too busy with your darts.

IRENE. Do you want me to stop on, Auntie Rhoda? 'Cause my Mam says I've got to try my dress on. 'Cause it's got to be shortened.

(RHODA *turns from the mounting argument with* EDGAR *and brings her mind to the immediate subject of the wedding.*)

RHODA. Well, what's she sent you down here for, if you're not going to do anything when you've come? Can't you just wipe them plates for me?

JACK. You what! Ask her to wipe your plates—she'll drop them.

IRENE. I don't drop them at all! I never drop them! When have you seen me drop plates?

JACK. No, you don't drop plates, do you? Have you got any money love? Lend us a quid.

IRENE. I haven't got a quid—and I wouldn't lend it to you if I had.

(JACK *darts across and picks up* IRENE'S *handbag which she has placed on the table.*)

JACK. Well, what have you got in here then?

IRENE (*unsuccessfully attempting to snatch back her handbag*). Hey, that's mine, when you've quite finished!

    (JACK *evades* IRENE *as she continues her attempts to regain the handbag.*)

JACK. There's two quid in here. Where did you get this from? I thought you didn't have any money?

IRENE. You just put it down! That's my personal property!

RHODA. Give up, our Jack! Leave her alone, for the last time of telling!

JACK (*taking a postcard-size photograph from the handbag*). Aye, aye!

    (IRENE *makes a grab for the photograph but* JACK *holds it up above his head and out of her reach.*)

Who's this then, eh?

IRENE. Nobody you know.

EDGAR (*to* JACK). Give up, dozy! Be your bloody age!

JACK (*still holding the photograph aloft, and reading the inscription*). "To Irene with lots of love from Stanley XXXX."

IRENE. You give that to me! You've no right to be looking at other people's things.

RHODA. Stop tormenting her, Jack. And just give her her handbag.

    (JACK *allows* IRENE *to snatch back the handbag.*)

EDGAR. Come on—stop mucking about!

    (JACK *lowers the photograph and again allows* IRENE *to snatch it from him.* IRENE *returns the photograph to the handbag as* JACK *speaks with exaggerated innocence.*)

JACK. What's up with you all? I'm just jealous, that's all. Where did you pick him up then, Irene?

IRENE. I didn't pick him up. I've known him for ages. He's a friend of Betty Rayner's, if it's anything to do with you.

JACK. You want to watch it you do—you want to be careful. 'Cause I've forked out for one wedding present this year—I'm not forking out for another.

RHODA. Do you want to be here till midnight all of you. 'Cause we're not coming back tomorrow morning, you know. You want to just get a move on and stop messing about.

IRENE. I can't stop late, Auntie Rhoda. I was just supposed to be bringing them knives down.

RHODA. Yes, well you can just finish them plates off. Your mother knows where you are.

    JACK *and* EDGAR *have returned to their task of grease-proofing the tables.* RHODA *returns to the crate where she removes the last of the crockery and* IRENE *wipes the dust from the plates.* EDGAR *presses home a drawing-pin and with* JACK *moves on to the next table.* JACK *attempts to enliven the conversation with a joke.)*

JACK. Hey, have you heard that one about this bloke? He gets stranded and he calls at this farmhouse to find out where he is?

EDGAR. Just watch what you're doing!

JACK. Anyway, this bird comes to the door in a dressing-gown. So. He thinks "Right! We're in!" So. He says, "Excuse me," he says, "I wonder if you can direct me on the road to Manchester, like!" So. Of course, this bird she's looking but she can't see him. Oh, I forgot to tell you, he's a little bloke. Only comes up to here. *(He puts out a hand.)* So. Of course, she looks and looks and she's got this parrot, like, on her shoulder.

*(*JACK *breaks off as the door opens and* ARTHUR BROADBENT *enters. He holds in his hand a pint of beer which he drains during the following conversation.)*

He's here! Watch your pockets! What are you doing up here, then? Won't they serve you down there?

*(*ARTHUR *pulls himself up before he speaks, which is his usual habit. He speaks slowly and ponderously as though making a great point of being sober.)*

ARTHUR. I've been downstairs. *(Still standing by the door he now opens it and calls down the stairs for confirmation.)* How long have I been standing downstairs, May? *(He allows the door to close without waiting for a reply.)* I've been in the passage. I've been standing down in that passage since seven o'clock. I thought you'd be coming down.

EDGAR. We were going to go down to the White Rose for one. We were going to finish off up here and then go down to the White Rose.

ARTHUR. You don't catch me at the White Rose. I've stopped going there. I can't get on with her. He's all right but I can't stand the sight of her. She can't take a joke.

RHODA. How much have you had tonight then?

*(*ARTHUR *ignores the question which does not interest him and, holding his empty glass, crosses to join* EDGAR *and* JACK.)*

ARTHUR. Do you know what she did? Have I to tell you why I fell out with her? Well, I'll tell you. I'd bought this joke. This plastic dog dirt. "Mucky Fido" it's called, you've got to laugh. So, of course, I slip it on the counter. She went mad. She did. She can't take a joke.

JACK. I'd like some of that for work. Hey, I say, you want to slip it on our lass's wedding cake!

EDGAR. So what does she do, then? Does she tell you to stop coming in?

ARTHUR. I won't go in! I wouldn't go in if it was the last pub in England!

JACK. You what! They'd have a job keeping you out if it was!

(ARTHUR *ignores this insult and, crossing and opening the door, calls down the stairs.*)

ARTHUR. Get them in, May, will you?

(RHODA, *however, realizing* ARTHUR'S *intentions, crosses and closes the door before* ARTHUR *has time to shout his order.*)

RHODA. Oh, but you don't! Oh, but you do not! We're having no drink up here.

ARTHUR. You don't begrudge me my only pleasure, do you, lass?

RHODA. I don't begrudge nobody nothing. It's not a matter of begrudging. I know you when you get started. I know you of old.

(ARTHUR *cheerfully accepts this denial and reprimand and calls across to* IRENE *as* RHODA *crosses to join her.*)

ARTHUR. Now then, love!

IRENE (*simpering back, pleased at being recognized by this elder of the family*). 'Lo, Uncle Arthur.

ARTHUR (*he studies* IRENE *for some moments meditatively*). My godfathers! She shoots up, that lass! She grows! She's a big one!

RHODA. I hope you've not come up here just to talk—'cause we've got work to do, if you did but know it.

ARTHUR. You're not having it all to do yourselves, are you? You know what you should have done, don't you? You should have got them people from Top Moor Side. They do it all for you.

EDGAR. Whittaker's. That's what I've been telling her. It's all on the cheap, is this. You can't do a job like this on the cheap.

RHODA. If you mention Whittaker's once more I'll brain you! (*Turning to* IRENE.) You can start laying the tables. And put the cups upside down so they won't get dust in them.

(IRENE *begins to place the cups and saucers on the tables which have already been covered with grease-proof paper.* ARTHUR *stands in the centre of the room and looks round with interest.*)

ARTHUR. Well, you've got it looking very nice. What's up with it? It's all right. Nothing wrong with that.

RHODA. It would be all right if we had a bit more help, and a bit less hindrance. And listen, just while I'm talking—I hope May doesn't think she's coming tomorrow, shaming us all up.

ARTHUR. Not her. Not May. Not that one. She keeps out of it.

(ARTHUR *crosses and sits by* JACK *and* EDGAR, *watching them at work.* RHODA *continues her remarks but without addressing them to anyone in particular.*)

RHODA. She does well to keep out of it. And I could name a lot more that keeps out of it when there's any work to be done. I wouldn't care but they promise to help. They swear blind they'll come down and give you a hand. Then they let you down. Then it's a case of: "Oooh, I forgot" or "Oooh, I was too busy". They won't be too busy to get their feet under the table tomorrow though.

(RHODA *pauses in her soliloquy as a thought takes hold of her. She glances round the room to confirm her suspicions before voicing them in more definite tones.*)

I've noticed one thing.

JACK (*addressing his father under his breath*). She's off.

RHODA. I've noticed one lot that isn't here. (*To* EDGAR.) Have you noticed anything? Just have a look round and tell me what you notice.

(EDGAR *looks round reluctantly—unwilling to be drawn in.*)

EDGAR. What?

RHODA. Just use your eyes. Have a look round and tell me what you notice. Go on!

(EDGAR *again glances round the room and attempts to find something unusual to remark on.*)

EDGAR. That grease-proof paper's too narrow.

RHODA. No! Who can't you see?

(EDGAR *is baffled and* JACK *tries to come to his rescue.*)

JACK. Well, that's a good one, is that! That's the best I've heard to-night! Who can't you see? Well, let's see, who can't I see? There's Prince Philip, I can't see him. Tony Hancock, he's not here. The Archbishop of Canterbury, Lester Piggott, Tommy Steele, Icky Plush—

RHODA (*interrupting*). You're so sharp you'll cut yourself one of these days. Anyway, I'm not talking to you. (*To* EDGAR.) I'll tell you who I've noticed isn't here. Well, who is here? There's only us.

(JACK *glances at the ceiling in despair.*)

There's only our side. There's only the bride's relations here. Nobody from the other side.

EDGAR. Well, it's our do, isn't it? I mean, that's what they say, isn't it? The bride's parents are responsible for the reception and the bridegroom's responsible for . . . well, for all the other side of it. He's got I don't know what to pay for.

RHODA. I've not mentioned paying. I can pay. I'm not short. It's just a question of helping out. I've not seen Bernard's mother for over a week.

IRENE (*glancing across*). I saw her, Auntie Rhoda. Do you know where

I saw her? I saw her walking up East End Road pushing a sack of coke in an old pram.

RHODA. She's not been near me. I don't even know how many she's got coming. She said fifteen but you don't know—it might be a hundred and fifteen.

(*The door opens and the bridegroom* BERNARD FULLER *enters.*)

BERNARD. Now then!

RHODA. Hello, Bernard. I was just saying, I've not seen your mother. Is she coming down, do you know?

BERNARD. Not that I know of.

JACK (*calling across the room*). How's Bernard then?

BERNARD. Not so bad.

JACK. Got any money then, Bernard? Lend us a quid?

BERNARD (*replying with slightly embarrassed jocularity*). I'm going to need all my money. (*Turning to* RHODA.) No, but I saw my Auntie Alice earlier on. She said she was coming round.

RHODA. Well, we've not seen her. I just passed the remark before you came in. I've not seen nobody from your side.

BERNARD (*sensing* RHODA'S *resentment*). Oh . . .

(ARTHUR *rises and crosses towards the door, pausing as he passes* BERNARD. ARTHUR *stops and gives* BERNARD *his long and contemplative look.*)

ARTHUR. You don't know me, do you?

BERNARD. I've seen your face.

ARTHUR. Yes, but you don't know me. I know you though. I've known you ever since you were a little lad. You ask your father if he knows me. Tell him Arthur Broadbent. He'll know that name.

BERNARD. Mr. Broadbent, yes, I will.

ARTHUR. No, say Arthur Broadbent. There's a lot of Broadbents round here.

(ARTHUR *turns and walks ponderously towards the door muttering beneath his breath the names of the fellow members of his clan.*)

Freddie Broadbent. Jack Broadbent, there's Harold Broadbent. There's two Harold Broadbents and there's them other Broadbents who live up the other side of Top Moor Park.

(ARTHUR *goes out through the door still mumbling to himself.* BERNARD *remains in the centre of the room for a moment feeling slightly an intruder and unsure of himself.* JACK *calls across to him.*)

JACK. Are you taking your coat off then, Bernard?

BERNARD (*reluctantly*). Why? What is there to do?

EDGAR. What is there to do, he says! It's a good job you don't get married every day! It is that! What is there to do! What isn't there to do!

RHODA. Yes, well you're not roping Bernard in. He'll be going out with his pals.

JACK (*making a pantomime of putting on his coat*). What? Are we going out then? I'm his pal. I'm your pal, aren't I, Bernard?

(BERNARD *grins self-consciously and crosses out of* JACK'S *range and towards* RHODA.)

BERNARD. I'm not having much to drink tonight, I'm not bothering. (*To* RHODA.) Is Christine coming down, Mrs. Lucas?

RHODA. You don't want Christine down. You want to keep out of her way. You know what they say—see the bride the night before, trouble will be forever at your door. That's what they say.

IRENE. Yes, they do, Auntie Rhoda. 'Cause we've got it in a book at home. It's got them all in—all these sayings. "Wedding cake beneath your head, dream of your true love in your bed." They gave it away in last week's *Diana*. This book. *The Diana Lucky Brides Book.* It's good, is *Diana*—'cause they give all sorts away.

(*The door opens and* ALICE FULLER *enters accompanied by* LILIAN HOWES.)

There's my Mam. Hello, Mam!

(ALICE *collapses into a chair in order to regain her breath as* LILIAN *approaches* IRENE *and* RHODA.)

LILIAN. What are you doing here? I thought I told you to come straight back?

RHODA. I asked her to stay. I couldn't be doing it all myself.

LILIAN (*to* IRENE). You do as your mother tells you in future. Not what other people tell you.

RHODA (*apparently ignoring this and turning to* ALICE *who is still struggling for breath*). Well, I'm glad somebody of Bernard's has come down— at long last. You're his Auntie Alice, aren't you?

ALICE (*speaking between deep gulps of breath*). Oh, I'm glad I don't live in an upstairs flat! I can't manage them stairs! Too much for me.

(ALICE *has now regained her breath and looks around the room critically.*)

It's a small room, isn't it? I've always said it was a small room. We've always used the Liberal Club, when we've had anything on. 'Cause I've always said: It's not how big the room looks it's when you've got your tables in.

RHODA. It's plenty big enough if they all sit down and don't wander about. It's big enough for what we want.

ALICE (*to* BERNARD). What are you doing here, our Bernard?

BERNARD. I just came in. I was on my way down to the "Rose" and I thought well I'll see how they're getting on.

ALICE. They shouldn't have let you in. I wouldn't have let you in.

(*To* RHODA.) I wouldn't have let him in, love. You know what they say: "See the bride the night before. . . ."

RHODA. Our Christine won't be down. She's like me, she's got a lot of work to do. (*She looks meaningly at* ALICE *and* LILIAN.) Now then, who hasn't got a job?

LILIAN. I'm just finding a brush. 'Cause this floor looks as if it could do with a good sweep.

(LILIAN *goes off in search of a brush as* RHODA *turns and stares obviously at* ALICE.)

RHODA. Right. Well, who does that leave then?

(ALICE *ignores the implied question and smiles good-humouredly at* RHODA.)

ALICE. Who's doing your catering, love?

RHODA. Barker's. (*She looks defiantly at* ALICE, *waiting for the criticism.*)

ALICE. Oh? Very nice. Yes, they're very reasonable. A lot of people don't like Barker's but I think they're very good. I've got nothing against Barker's. 'Cause you've nothing to pay for except the food—what you eat. You've no waitresses to pay for. Well, you don't want waitresses when you're among yourselves. I mean, you just muck in, don't you?

RHODA (*beginning to take umbrage at these patronizing remarks*). There's no question of mucking in. I've got a neighbour coming in to very kindly pour the tea. Everything else will be laid out—on the plates—your salad and that, and you've got your cake and your sweet in the middle. So you don't need a waitress.

ALICE (*nodding benignly and again glancing around the room*). Well, you do right, love. No sense in chucking your money about, because they don't appreciate it. They don't send you table-cloths then? Barker's?

(RHODA *turns away from* ALICE *and returns to the table and begins to sort the knives and forks from the tray.* LILIAN *has found a brush and is sweeping the floor.* EDGAR *and* JACK, *who are taking their time, are still covering the tables with grease-proof paper.* IRENE *is meticulously laying out cups and saucers on the covered tables.* BERNARD, *still at a loose end, is merely hanging about. The door opens and* ARTHUR *enters carrying a nearly full pint glass of beer.* JACK *glances across at* ARTHUR *and calls out sarcastically.*)

JACK. You're all right then, Arthur? You got your pint in? S'all right, don't bother about us! He's a good lad, is Arthur!

(ARTHUR, *holding his pint at chest-level, turns ponderously towards* JACK. *He replies good-humouredly.*)

ARTHUR. You what? Haven't you got one then? Well, I don't know. You should have said. I thought you were working.

JACK. By bloody hell! Hey, Bernard! He could give you lessons.

BERNARD (*looking at* JACK, *eager to please*). Do you want a pint, Jack? I'll buy you a pint. Anyway, I must owe you a pint by now.

(BERNARD *steps backward awkwardly, almost falling, as he trips over* LILIAN'*s brush.*)

LILIAN. Be careful, young man! Mind yourself! I'm trying to get swept up!

BERNARD. I'm sorry.

(BERNARD *crosses unhappily into a corner of the room as* LILIAN *sweeps the floor and approaches* IRENE. IRENE *is now laying out small plates in each place.*)

LILIAN. What are you doing, you great Mary Ann!

IRENE. Hello, Mam! I'm putting these plates out.

LILIAN. I can see you are—you're putting them in the wrong place. You want knife and fork plates where you're putting them. These are what you call your bread and butter plates. For your bread and butter and everything you have after—like cake or a bun or anything like that.

IRENE. Well, where's the knife and fork plates then?

LILIAN. I don't know. They're not my plates. (*Calling across to* RHODA.) Rhoda! Where's your big plates?

RHODA (*crossing to join them*). What big plates?

LILIAN. Well, your big plates—for your salad. Your knife and fork plates.

(RHODA *thinks for a moment before answering.* ALICE *crosses and joins the group.*)

RHODA. Well, there's only that one case. It's funny how you don't notice, isn't it? 'Cause I unpacked it myself and I never thought. They must be sending them round tomorrow with the food.

ALICE. Not if it's Barker's, love. It's only sandwiches that you get, love. 'Cause otherwise they'd have sent you knives and forks, wouldn't they? You wouldn't have had to fetch your own.

RHODA. 'Course it's not sandwiches. It's a salad.

(EDGAR *crosses to join the group.*)

LILIAN. Well, are you sure it's a salad? Did you ask them if it was a salad?

RHODA. It's always a salad. Weddings. They don't push you off with sandwiches for a wedding. You don't tell me they're charging three-and-six a head for a sandwich.

EDGAR. Well, you must have asked them—what they're going to give you?

LILIAN. She wouldn't have thought to ask.

EDGAR. Well, I'm going to ask. I'm going to ring them up. Who's got four pennies?

ALICE. You've no need to ring them up if it's Barker's. I've been to dozens of their do's. Dozens. Dozens and dozens. I've lost count. I can tell you what you'll get, love. You'll get your little itsy-bitsy three-cornered sandwich. (*She indicates with thumb and forefinger.*) You get two of them each. And either you get your custard slice or your chocolate marshmallow. But you don't get both. And there's your cake, and that's it. (*Suddenly raising her voice decisively.*) No salad! There's no salad! They won't do salads, won't Barker's. If you want salads you have to go to Whittaker's.

EDGAR. On the cheap! You see, you won't be told! On the flaming cheap!

(EDGAR *turns in disgust and moves away; he pauses for a moment to call over his shoulder.*)

EDGAR. They'll just have to go hungry till they get home—all of them!

RHODA (*too crumpled to reply to* EDGAR). Oh, dear me, oh, dear me . . .

IRENE. What have I to do with these plates, Mam?

(BERNARD *crosses to join the group.*)

LILIAN. We'll need plates—whatever they give us.

ALICE. Well, don't go banking on salad. 'Cause they don't do salads, Barker's. I know that.

(ALICE *moves away and returns to her chair.*)

BERNARD (*helpfully*). Well, we'll manage—we're not bothered. As long as there's a bit of cake each, that's all you want. A bit of cake and a cup of tea.

LILIAN. Well, you might but there's more than you to consider. There's some people coming a long way for this.

(LILIAN *moves away and resumes her sweeping energetically.* RHODA *has recovered her composure sufficiently to vent her feelings on* LILIAN. *She calls out to her.*)

RHODA. Don't go lifting that dust all over the cups. We've got to drink out of them when you've finished.

IRENE. Well, what have I to do about these plates, Aunt Rhoda?

RHODA. Oh, I've got more to bother about than plates, love. Don't worry me now.

(IRENE *shrugs indifferently and moves away to continue laying out the plates.* BERNARD *crosses towards* JACK. RHODA *stands alone amidst all the activity for some moments before* EDGAR *crosses to rejoin her. They speak in almost confidential tones.*)

EDGAR. You see, I tried to tell you. But you get an idea in your head and there's no shifting it. Where did I tell you to go? Right from the very beginning?

RHODA. Oh, well, it's too late now. I'm past caring.

EDGAR (*quiet but persistent*). You see, it shows us up. I mean, there's your Frank. I can just picture him going home and saying, "Well, I pity them if that's all they can give us."

RHODA. If our Frank doesn't like it he can do the other thing.

EDGAR. You see, there you go. You don't think. I mean, he does enough for you, your Frank. He's putting himself out tomorrow—it's his busy day Saturday and he's letting you have both his taxis. Then there's your holidays—he always drives you to Scarborough. Always. Well, when you invite him to a wedding you don't do it on the cheap.

RHODA. Well, if you knew all about it, why didn't you do it? It's me that's had all the chasing about to do. No good getting on to me now.

EDGAR. Nobody's getting on at you, love. I'm just saying, you want to listen to people.

(RHODA *knows she is in the wrong but is not in the habit of admitting it.*)

RHODA. Yes—well you want to listen to people as well.

(RHODA *breaks off as the door opens and* CHRISTINE LUCAS, *the bride, enters, carrying two large and flimsy white boxes which contain the wedding cake. There is an immediate stunned silence from the occupants of the room at the awful significance of this meeting of the bride and groom. The silence is broken by* IRENE *who, clapping her hand to her mouth, speaks in a frightened voice.*)

IRENE. Oooh, Mother!

LILIAN (*to* CHRISTINE). Hey, get out! Don't you know who's here?

ALICE. It's too late now, love. She's seen him now. The damage is done.

(BERNARD *and* CHRISTINE *hold each other's glance across the room.* CHRISTINE'S *first expression of alarm quickly dispels and she smiles at* BERNARD—*the smile is returned.*)

CHRISTINE. What are you doing here?

BERNARD. What are you doing here?

CHRISTINE. I've brought the cake down.

RHODA. Well, you've done it now, the pair of you.

(CHRISTINE *comes into the room, allowing the door to close behind her.*)

CHRISTINE. We haven't done anything, what are you talking about?

RHODA. You know what they say. "See the bride the night before . . ."

CHRISTINE (*easily*). Oh, it's only superstition, is that.

(*The tension is relaxed, and further broken by* JACK *as he crosses to take the boxes from* CHRISTINE.)

JACK. Is this my present, our lass?

CHRISTINE. How do you mean—your present?

JACK. It's a new custom I've just invented: the bride's brother always gets a present.

(CHRISTINE *gives* JACK *a deprecatory gesture as he moves to place the cake-boxes on the table.* CHRISTINE *crosses to* BERNARD.)

CHRISTINE. Hello, Bernard.

BERNARD. Hello, Christine.

CHRISTINE. You've had your hair cut then?

BERNARD. Yeh, I went this afternoon. I finished work at dinner-time and I went straight in on my way home. There were only two other blokes in.

CHRISTINE. Looks a bit better than it did yesterday. You needed a hair-cut you did.

BERNARD. Yeh. I went to Carter's. Don't usually go there.

CHRISTINE. It looks all right.

BERNARD. I usually go somewhere else.

CHRISTINE. You're lucky. I've got to rush out tomorrow morning to get mine done.

BERNARD. You're not having your hair done, are you?

CHRISTINE. 'Course I am, you daft devil. Don't think I'm getting married with it like this, do you?

BERNARD. Well, don't get it cut short then. I don't like it short.

CHRISTINE. You just wait and see.

(BERNARD *and* CHRISTINE *sit together quietly while the activity grows around them. There is a mood of closeness between them but* BERNARD *cannot think of anything to say. His mind is working desperately.*)

BERNARD. You didn't go to work today, did you?

CHRISTINE. I didn't go to work, but I called in. Ooh, you want to see what they've given us!

BERNARD. What?

CHRISTINE. Well, two things. Well, only one thing really. A water set.

BERNARD. A what?

CHRISTINE. You know—jug and six glasses. It's in green. I think it's lovely. And they've given us a toilet roll.

BERNARD. You what?

CHRISTINE. You know—well, it was just a laugh. 'Cause Barbara Warburton and Maureen went out to buy the present, and they had about a shilling left over.

BERNARD (*politely*). Oh, yes?

(*Again the conversation lapses into a comfortable silence.* ALICE *crosses and addresses* CHRISTINE.)

ALICE. Excuse me for asking, love, but is that your cake you've just brought in?

CHRISTINE. Yes, why?

ALICE. Would it be asking too much if I had a look at it?

CHRISTINE. No, you can have a look at it. Haven't you seen it? It's been in Barker's window.

ALICE. No, well you see, love, I never go down that end. I go to Mainprice's when I want anything.

(CHRISTINE *rises and, followed by* ALICE *and* BERNARD, *crosses to the table and opens the cake-box.* CHRISTINE *takes out the large cake and the supporting pillars.*)

Oh, yes! Very nice. Very nice indeed. It is nice is that.

(CHRISTINE *places the smaller cake on top and places a small model of a bridegroom in the centre.*)

CHRISTINE. Do you like it?

ALICE. I think it's very nice. I think they've done a very good job.

(IRENE *crosses to join them and her eyes fasten on the cake.*)

IRENE. Oooh, Mam! Come and have a look! Quick!

LILIAN (*coming over to look at the cake*). What do you mean, "quick"? It's not going to melt, is it?

(*The other people in the room cross to view the cake.* ARTHUR, *still holding his empty glass, pushes his way to the front.*)

ARTHUR. By gow! That'll take some eating. I say, that'll take some eating!

IRENE. I like your statues. You'll be able to save them.

EDGAR. Yes, very nice.

JACK (*jokingly putting out his hand*). Well, come on, our lass, get it cut. Aren't we having a slice?

CHRISTINE. You get your mucky hands off it.

RHODA (*flashing* ALICE *a baleful glance*). You want to get it covered up. People breathing on it.

(ALICE *takes this as a personal insult—which, indeed, it is.*)

ALICE. It's all right, love. It's got icing round it. They keep for years, wedding cakes. Years and years.

RHODA. Doesn't matter how long they keep. You don't want it all covered in dust.

ALICE. Well, you know what they say: we've all got to eat so much muck before we die.

(ALICE's *bitterly sweet fixed smile is being met by* RHODA's *cold stare—the impending argument, however, is dispelled as the door opens and* EDNA FULLER *enters.*)

EDNA. Have I come to the right shop?

CHRISTINE (*to* BERNARD). Here's your mother.

(RHODA *crosses to greet* EDNA *with the formality befitting the head of the opposite family.*)

RHODA. You managed to get down then?

EDNA. Only just. I've been sitting in front of the fire all night. I can't get warm. I sit in front of that fire, I'm roasting on one side—I'm like a block of ice on the other. And if I sit too near I get pins and needles. It starts up here. (*She indicates her shoulder.*) And it goes right down there. (*She runs her hand down her arm.*)

EDGAR (*crossing to greet her*). How you keeping then, love?

EDNA. Very well, thank you. (*Continuing her discourse to* RHODA.) And I can't bend.

RHODA (*breaking in hastily*). We were just looking at the cake. It's come out very nice.

(RHODA, EDNA *and* EDGAR *cross to join the group round the cake. The group parts to allow* EDNA *a view of the cake.* EDNA *appraises the cake silently for some moments.*)

EDNA. You decided on the two-tier then? In the finish?

CHRISTINE. Well, we thought so. We thought about a three-tier then we thought, well, we'll have two. It's enough.

BERNARD. I mean, you don't have a big fat wedge out, Mother. You only have a thin slice.

EDNA. I don't know whether I shall have any. It's too rich for me—wedding cake. It upsets my stomach. Then I go for days and days. I have nothing except a glass of water.

IRENE. They're all the go these days: two-tier cakes. I saw one in last week's *Shirley*. It's what that rich blackie princess had that got married to Dean Sexton.

(RHODA *decides that this idle conversation has gone on too long and redirects them back to their tasks briskly.*)

RHODA. Well, let's see now. Who's doing what? (*To* EDGAR *and* JACK.) If you two have finished them tables there's the chairs want putting out. (*To* IRENE.) Irene can be finishing the plates, love. (*To* LILIAN.) You're doing the sweeping-up? (*To* ALICE.) Then there's Bernard's Auntie. We haven't given you a job, have we, love? Who wants to go round with a duster?

ALICE. I'll do your bit of dusting for you, love. Might as well be doing something.

(*They return to their designated tasks.* CHRISTINE *also gives a hand about the room, followed aimlessly by* BERNARD *with his hands in his pockets.* ARTHUR, *pint glass in hand, continues to gaze stolidly and benevolently about the room.* RHODA *turns to* EDNA.)

RHODA. We'd better just have a sit down and work out who's coming. Because there's four or five on your side we haven't heard a word from.

(RHODA *and* EDNA *sit down facing each other.*)

EDNA. No, and you won't either—some of them. There's our Walter, I've asked him time and time again if he's coming. But you can't get any sense out of him. He keeps saying: "Well, I think so. I think so."

RHODA. Well, it's no use him thinking so. Is he coming or isn't he?

EDNA. Well, they're all coming—so far as I know. Except our Walter —I can't swear for him. And there's our Jenny. She won't be here. You know she won't be here, don't you?

RHODA. Well, I don't know, you see. That's what I don't know. Which is your Jenny?

EDNA. You do know our Jenny. You know her to look at. She goes in the Rose a lot.

RHODA. No . . . No . . . I can't place her.

EDNA. Anyway, she can't come for one. The other one I can't vouch for is our Miriam.

RHODA. You see, we should have got all this settled. It's throwing us all out.

EDNA. I know. I know, love. I know what it's like. I've been down and I've been down and she's never in. I've knocked on the window. And you can't keep on going down. It does me no good. 'Cause I know just as soon as I get back in that house I have to lie down.

RHODA. Anyway, you've got fifteen coming? Definite?

EDNA. I don't know whether it's fourteen or fifteen or sixteen or what it is.

(RHODA *sits back in despair and shakes her head.* ARTHUR, *his pint glass still poised at chest-level though empty, approaches* RHODA *and* EDNA.)

ARTHUR (*to* EDNA). How you keepin' then, missis?

EDNA (*not recognizing* ARTHUR, *she replies politely*). Very well, thank you.

ARTHUR. You don't know me, do you? I can see you studying.

EDNA. Well, I've seen you somewhere, I know that.

ARTHUR. I know you've seen me somewhere, but you don't know where, do you? Just you ask your husband when you get home. Tell him you've seen Arthur.

EDNA. It's Mr. Broadbent, isn't it?

ARTHUR (*staring at* EDNA *and inscrutably refusing to give anything away*). Just tell him you've seen Arthur. No, I'll tell you what! Just say "Mucky Fido" to him. That's all. See what he says. Watch his face.

RHODA. We don't want any of your tricks and games tomorrow—so think on.

ARTHUR (*cheerfully*). I shall be too busy tomorrow. I've got to go down there.

(RHODA *looks at him suspiciously.* EDNA *simpers tolerantly.*)

RHODA. Down where? What are you talking about?

ARTHUR (*realizing he has revealed his true intentions and beginning to tread very cautiously*). Where I always go on a Saturday. Down to the Paternoster's Arms for half an hour. It's the Lodge Meeting.

RHODA. Well, you're not going to the Lodge tomorrow.

ARTHUR. I shall only go in for half an hour.

RHODA. Half an hour till when? You know the service starts at two o'clock.

ARTHUR (*treading more cautiously than ever*). No, well. If I miss you up there I'll see you down here.

RHODA. Well, what arrangements have you made about our Frank picking you up in the car?

ARTHUR. I told him not to bother. I can make my own way.

RHODA. Well, we don't want you rolling in here at three o'clock and saying you missed the service.

ARTHUR. I shall make my own way—I shall make my own arrangements. I'll get there somehow, sometime.

(ARTHUR *looks vaguely about the room and wanders away disinclined to continue the conversation, leaving* RHODA *disturbed.*)

RHODA (*to* EDNA). You see, you don't know where you stand with any of them.

EDNA. Just like our Walter. I know where I've seen him before now. Our Geoffrey fetched him home one night. They'd been down to the barracks the pair of them. There was them two and a sergeant-major. Well, he was incapable. They'd won this bottle of green stuff. They'd won it. And they stayed up all night supping it and doing conjuring tricks.

RHODA. I'm frightened of what he's going to say when he comes in tomorrow. You never know what he'll come out with when he's had a few.

EDNA. Our Walter's just the same.

RHODA. Oh, while I'm thinking! (*She calls across to* EDGAR.) Edgar!

EDGAR (*calling back*). What, love?

RHODA. What about glasses for the toast?

BERNARD. Our Lionel's fetching them down.

CHRISTINE. Oh, and don't think you're going to get drunk tomorrow.

BERNARD (*with a forced laugh*). You don't have to worry about me, love.

CHRISTINE. I don't worry about you. But I don't want you looking like that night when our Jack took you playing billiards. Because we'll want you sober tomorrow—you'll have your speech to make.

BERNARD (*with alarm*). What speech?

CHRISTINE. Well, your speech. You've got to toast the bridesmaids.

BERNARD. I'm not toasting no bridesmaids. Who do you think I am?

CHRISTINE. You're supposed to be the bridegroom, if you did but know it. They always make a speech—bridegrooms.

BERNARD. Well, I'm not making one. I don't care what they do—I'm not making one.

CHRISTINE (*calling across to* JACK). Hey, our Jack!

JACK. What?

CHRISTINE. You tell Bernard he's got to make a speech, he doesn't believe me.

JACK (*crosses to* CHRISTINE *and* BERNARD). Well, didn't you know you have to make a speech, Bernard? 'Course you have. I'm off to make one.

CHRISTINE. You're not, you know.

JACK. I've got it all ready. I'm going to tell them a joke. Hey, Bernard, have you heard that one? There's this bloke knocks on this farmhouse door and this tart comes out in a dressing-gown with this parrot. And he's only as big as this— (*He gestures.*) this bloke.

CHRISTINE. We're not having you telling your mucky jokes. So you can get that idea out of your head. It's all arranged, who's making speeches and who isn't. There's your bridegroom's speech, there's your best man's speech, and Uncle Arthur's making his speech.

ARTHUR (*modestly*). You don't want to hear my speech again, do you?

CHRISTINE. 'Course we do. We always have your speech.

ARTHUR. I've forgotten it. I haven't done it since Christmas. How does it go now? (ARTHUR *pauses, considers, clears his throat and raises his empty glass still higher as he announces the title of his speech.*) "What is Marriage?" (*He pauses.*) "Marriage is an institution no family should be without."

   (*As* ARTHUR *continues with his set-piece, the remaining occupants of the room leave their tasks and gather round to listen admiringly.*) "Marriage is a company made in Heaven which has two directors. The husband is the chairman and the treasurer and the wife is the managing director and the . . . and the . . ." (*He thinks again.*) Wait a minute, I used to have this off pat. (*He thinks again.*) "Marriage is annoying, frustrating, a worry, a nuisance, a millstone around our necks but we wouldn't be without it." (*He thinks again.*) "Only fools marry but only fools stay single."

ALICE. You've missed out the best part, love.

RHODA (*turns to* ALICE *and speaks in a forceful whisper, not wishing to disturb* ARTHUR's *train of thought*). He knows what he's saying. He's been doing it for years.

ALICE. Oh, I know, love. I've heard him. Many a time. That's why I'm saying. He's missed out that bit about "the marriage bed may be lumpy".

RHODA. Let him get on with it.

ARTHUR. "A man without a wife is like a ship without a rudder drifting hopelessly on the turbulent sea of life . . ." (*He thinks again.*) Now then, how the bloody hell does it go now?

(*They are waiting quietly and respectfully for* ARTHUR *to continue as the door opens and* FRANK BROADBENT *enters.*)

FRANK (*sarcastically*). Aye, aye! Hard at it?

RHODA. It's the first break we've had all night. I'll tell you.

FRANK. Now then, Arthur! I was looking for you down there.

ARTHUR. I haven't had a chance—I've been working.

JACK (*crossing to join the group as they disperse to continue with their appointed tasks*). Lend us a quid, Frank.

FRANK. I wish I had one to lend you. I could do with one myself.

JACK. Don't give us that. You must be coining it.

FRANK (*turns to* ARTHUR, *dismissing* JACK *who joins* EDGAR *at the tables*). No, only I was trying to get that there for you. He came in, you know—Sidney Jeffries. He says the best he can do for you is sprouts. But he'll have a red cabbage for you tomorrow, when you see him.

ARTHUR. That's twice he's sent somebody round with that tale. I'll believe it when I see it. He's been promising me that red cabbage for I don't know how long.

FRANK. He's going down the allotment tomorrow—making a special trip. He'll have it for you.

RHODA (*who has been trying to draw* FRANK'S *attention, is incensed at these remarks which she has overheard. To* ARTHUR). Listen, you're not going traipsing round with a red cabbage under your arm tomorrow.

ARTHUR. No, I shall take a carrier-bag down.

RHODA. You're not going in that church with a carrier-bag.

ARTHUR. Well, that's just the question. Whether I can get there. You see, if I have to wait for him it's going to be a bit of a rush.

RHODA. Well, I've finished bothering. I don't care whether you come or not. But if you do come you're not fetching any carrier-bag.

(RHODA *turns impatiently away from* ARTHUR *who undisturbed drifts away across the room to watch the work which has been resumed.* RHODA *turns to* FRANK. FRANK *has been looking around at the general proceedings and now speaks rather patronizingly.*)

FRANK. Yes, well it's looking very nice, to say.

RHODA. It'll be all right when we've got them all sat down.

FRANK. Is this how you're keeping your tables then?

RHODA. How do you mean? What's wrong with them?

FRANK. There's nothing wrong with them. I'm not criticizing. I mean, it's up to you, how you have them.

RHODA. Well, how else can you have them?

FRANK. Have them how you like, love. How it suits you. Only if it were me I'd have my top table, you see.

RHODA (*comprehending immediately*). Oh, yes!

FRANK. You see, you have your top table where you have your bride and your groom and your cake and that—your best man. Then you have your two flanks—what we call flanks—coming down, where you sit your guests in order of precedence.

RHODA (*turns and calls urgently across the room*). Edgar!

(EDGAR *crosses to join* RHODA *and* FRANK.)

FRANK. You see, otherwise you get people sitting all over the shop. (EDGAR *arrives.*) I'm just saying, Edgar. You want a top table.

EDGAR. Top table?

RHODA. You remember! Like when we went to Marion's wedding. How they had the tables then.

EDGAR. That's just how they had them. You don't always have them like that.

FRANK. Well, that's what you do, apparently. You see, apparently you always have it like that. You never have it any other way. Not for weddings. (*A thought strikes him and he shouts excitedly.*) Except Moslem weddings!

RHODA. Never mind about Moslem weddings. We'll have to get these tables rearranged.

EDGAR. We've got them all set out now.

RHODA. Well, you can just get them set out again. Like you saw them at Marion's wedding. That's your job before you do anything else.

(EDGAR *moves off shaking his head despairingly, during the following dialogue he enlists the help of* JACK, BERNARD *and* IRENE *and begins to instruct them in placing the tables.* RHODA *returns to her conversation with* FRANK.)

We could have done with you a bit sooner.

FRANK. Ah, well, I've had a lot of dashing about to do. See, a lot of people think you've got it cushy when you work for yourself. They don't stop to consider. I've had a hell of a day. I've had to go out myself. Got a driver off sick. Young Leslie—you know Leslie— well, he's badly.

RHODA. You'll be all right for tomorrow with the taxis, won't you?

FRANK. That's what I called in about. I shall be all right—touch wood —in one sense. But you see, there's been a bit of a mix-up.

RHODA (*looking at* FRANK *suspiciously*). Oh, dear me.

FRANK. You see, you've heard me talk of Micky Patterson, haven't you?

RHODA. Micky who?

FRANK. Well, don't tell me you don't know who Micky Patterson is! He's only the Loose Forward for the City, that's all. He's played for the first team every match this year.

RHODA. I don't bother with football.

FRANK. You've heard me talk of him. Well, I know him very well indeed. I've bought him a drink—many a time. Anyway, what it boils down to is we're in a bit of a turmoil. You see, I always drive Patterson to the match—when they're playing at home. I drive him myself—always have done.

RHODA (*coldly*). Oh, yes.

FRANK. Yes. Well, you see, there's been a bit of a turmoil with the booking-sheets.

RHODA (*calling across the room*). Edgar!

    (EDGAR *crosses to join* RHODA *and* FRANK *as* BERNARD, JACK *and* IRENE *begin to rearrange the tables.*)

FRANK. You see, I'd got him booked down for the first and fifteenth of this month and the fifth of next month. Well, course, what it should have been is the first, fifteenth and twenty-ninth. Well, of course, that's tomorrow. So, of course, we clash. (*He pauses from a torrent of words.*) I'm just saying, Edgar. Young Leslie's mullocksed all the sheets up. He's got your wedding down but he's not booked Patterson to the ground.

EDGAR. Well, how do we stand then?

RHODA. I'll be glad when this wedding's over.

FRANK. No, well it's all right. Fortunately. Because, fortunately, we've been able to work out a new schedule.

EDGAR (*still grateful for* FRANK's *aid under any circumstances he hastens to reassure him*). As long as we're not putting you out.

FRANK. No, you're not putting me out. Far from it. You see, it's Patterson, Edgar. You see, he's a very good customer. I lose him I lose a lot of mileage.

RHODA. Well, how do we stand then?

EDGAR. Well, he's just saying—he doesn't like to let nobody down. He'll do the best he can.

FRANK. Right. Now you see, what we'd arranged is that we have one car X.U.B., goes to your house, journeys to the church; return— wait—and takes the bride. Right?

EDGAR (*nodding*). I'm with you. X.U.B.

FRANK. Right. Then he goes round to Delaney Street and fetches them others. Then we've got W.W.T. He's picking up Bernard's lot—journey to church—return twice.

EDGAR. W.W.T. I've got it.

FRANK. Yes, well, we can't do that. 'Cause you see, it's on the sheets for X.U.B. to pick up Patterson. Naturally that alters the circumstances.

EDGAR. Well, it will do.

FRANK. Right. Now are you listening? Now, in the circumstances, what we'll do is X.U.B. will do the round trip. You see, he'll have several ports of call. You see, first of all he picks up Patterson and they're going down there to pick up a chicken.

EDGAR. Oh, yes.

FRANK. To take round to his mother's. 'Cause he takes her a chicken round every week. Always has done. Now then, he'll stop at his mother's for half an hour—that gives X.U.B. chance to dash back and get four of you into the church. They'll be there if nobody else is, 'cause they'll be there half an hour early. Then he'll have to dash back, pick up Patterson, and take him on to the ground. Right, so far, so good. Now then, he's going to be too late then to pick up the bride. So what we'll have to do, we'll have to press W.W.T. into service earlier on. He's only got a station job on, one fifteen. So, soon as he gets round to you, you give him a hand to whip his ribbons on and you're away, all of you.

RHODA. Well, what about Bernard's family?

FRANK. Ah, well, this is where we've got to keep our fingers crossed. You see, as soon as X.U.B.'s finished with Patterson he dashes down to what's his name's, Bernard's. And takes them. We hope. But, you see, he'll only have time to take one load. Now, it comes to this —is any of them going to mind going in a van?

RHODA (*heatedly*). I'm not going in a van!

FRANK (*patiently*). No, you haven't understood, love. You're going in X.U.B. You're going in the limousine. It's just a question of getting the last few people mopped up. 'Cause we'll be pressed for time. You see, I've got the little van—it's clean—it's doing nothing—it's just a question of whether anybody's going to mind.

RHODA. It's not for us to say, is it? We're not going to ride in it. But I know I'd object—I'd object most strongly—if it was me. Better have a word with Bernard's mother. (*She calls to* EDNA.) Mrs. Fuller! Have you a minute?

    (EDNA *crosses and joins* RHODA *and* FRANK. *She looks at* RHODA *inquiringly*.)

FRANK. No, we were just saying, love. We're in a bit of a turmoil over the cars. I was just wondering if one or two of your younger ones would object to journeying in a small clean van?

EDNA (*not at all taken aback at the ethics of travelling in a small clean van*). I can't do with vans. You get all this smell of petrol in your lungs. It makes me sick. I've only to get down as far as the bottom of the street and I've to get out and walk round.

FRANK. No, it's not you, love. You'll be going in the car. You're all right.

EDNA. I'm the same in a car. Whether it's a car or a van or a bus or a tram or what it is. I've to get out and walk round.

FRANK. Anyway, there's some of the younger ones. They won't mind. They'll like it. It's all experience.

EDGAR. It'll all come out all right in the wash.

FRANK. Oh, it's nothing to what we do have. (FRANK *dismissing the subject, glances across at the tables which by now, are well on the way to being reassembled.*) That's more like. That's one hundred per cent improvement. You know what you're doing now. (*He glances at his watch.*) Anyway, I won't stop, Rhoda. I've got to get up there.

RHODA. Well, we're all right for tomorrow, are we?

FRANK (*crossing to the door*). Let me worry about that. So, I'll see you tomorrow—God willing. We'll sort something out. G'night, Arthur! G'night, Jack!

(FRANK *exits.* RHODA *gives* JACK *a worried glance.* EDNA *turns to* RHODA.)

EDNA. He's got on, hasn't he? Your Frank.

EDGAR. He's done very well for himself. It's all hard work, you know. All hard graft.

RHODA. He takes too much on, that's all that's wrong with him. He tries to do too much. I'm only praying he's not bitten off more than he can chew tomorrow.

EDGAR. He's never let you down yet.

RHODA. Depends what you mean by "let you down".

EDNA (*to* RHODA). Our Alice says you've decided against salad then?

RHODA. It's not a matter of deciding. It was decided for us. It's the last time I go to Barker's, I know that.

EDNA. I don't like Barker's. 'Cause I said when our Bernard told me you were going there. I said, well, I wouldn't have gone there if it had been left to me. 'Cause don't you remember that case they had against them? When they had them up. That time when a woman found a bit of mucky bandage in a cream horn. They got fined. Guilty.

RHODA. Oh, that's ages ago. That was old Mr. Barker. They've got it all tiled now.

(*The door opens and* LIONEL *and* MARGO FULLER *enter, carrying between them a large box containing a newspaper-wrapped motley collection of small glasses.*)

LIONEL. I hope you'll excuse us barging in on you. We couldn't knock, we had our hands full.

RHODA. Oh, you take no notice here, lad. Come in as you please, we don't mind.

LIONEL. We've brought your glasses down for you.

(LIONEL *and* MARGO *lower the case to the floor.*)

EDNA (*to* RHODA). You know this lad, don't you? Our Alice's boy, Lionel. Best man.

RHODA. I've seen him knocking about.

LIONEL (*approaches and elaborately fully extends his arm to shake hands with* RHODA). Pleased to meet you. (*He turns to* EDGAR.) Pleased to meet you. (*He turns to* EDNA.) How are you keeping then, Auntie Edna? Are you any better?

EDNA. I'm managing.

LIONEL. You're looking better.

MARGO (*thumps* LIONEL—*her usual manner of drawing his attention*). She's over there, your mother.

(MARGO *indicates* ALICE, *and* LIONEL *shambles across to speak to his mother, addressing "Good evenings" to whoever he passes.* MARGO *turns to* RHODA.)

I'm not speaking to his mother and she's not speaking to me. So that makes two of us.

RHODA. Oh, I'm sorry to hear that.

MARGO (*casually*). Doesn't bother me. She can go and take a running jump at herself, for all I care. I hope she drops dead tomorrow.

EDNA. You shouldn't say things like that, love. How would you feel if she got knocked down in the morning?

MARGO. Wouldn't worry me.

RHODA. You want to be careful what you're saying. You might have need of her one of these days.

MARGO (*ignores this and calls across the room to* LIONEL *who is still talking to his mother*). Lionel! Are you going to get these glasses unpacked?

LIONEL (*calling across the room*). I'll be with you in a minute, love.

MARGO. We're supposed to be going out, when you've quite finished.

LIONEL. I'm coming. (*Turning to* ALICE *and continuing his conversation.*) No, 'cause we only called in. We're supposed to be meeting Hetty and George at the Roebuck Arms.

ALICE (*glancing at* MARGO *distastefully*). She's not going to go up to Roebuck looking like that, is she?

LIONEL. She's all right. We're not going in the best room.

ALICE. Well, you please yourself. But I wouldn't be seen out with her. What's she done about tomorrow? Has she bought herself a pair of shoes yet?

LIONEL. I gave her the money for a pair last week but she comes home with a cake-stand.

ALICE. Well, if she walks into the church tomorrow in them old black shoes I walk out.

LIONEL. Well, what can you do? She's had the money. Only she saw this cake-stand—and it's very nice. We needed one. What can you say?

(BERNARD *crosses to join* LIONEL.)

ALICE. Well, you know what they've started calling her—Mucky Margo.

LIONEL. I take no notice of that. They can say what they like.' (*He turns as* BERNARD *arrives.*) Now then, Bernard! Are you feeling nervous?

BERNARD. I'm all right, Lionel. Are you all right, that's what I want to know.

LIONEL. I'll be there, don't worry.

BERNARD. Have you got fixed up with Ken Frazer yet?

LIONEL. Not since last Sunday—he was all right then. I'm going down first thing in the morning.

ALICE. Hey! He's not taking your wedding photos is he, Ken Frazer?

BERNARD. I hope he is. It's all fixed up, isn't it?

LIONEL. Well, he said he was coming. That's what he told me last Sunday morning. I bumped into him—he was going up to his mother's. Only we couldn't talk 'cause he'd got all the kiddies with him. He'd got their Freda and their Laurence in the pram. He'd got Susan on a little three-wheeler bike. And little Boris pulling a Sooty on wheels. So, you can tell, he had his hands full.

ALICE. Have you got it in writing? What he's going to do? He's unreliable, you know that?

BERNARD. He's all right. I know him. I used to work with him. If he says he'll come, he'll come. I mean it's all money in his pocket, isn't it?

ALICE. I say he's unreliable, love. He'll be late for his own funeral will that one. (*She turns to* LIONEL.) Well, you know! He let you down. You know very well he let you down.

LIONEL. Well, he came didn't he?

ALICE. Yes, he came. He came at four o'clock when we were half-way through the reception. And then what had you to do? We all had to go trooping back to the church in all that rain and pretend to be just coming out.

BERNARD. It's been fixed up for ages, has this.

JACK (*crossing to join the group*). Give us a fag, Bernard.

    (BERNARD *absentmindedly holds out a cigarette packet to* JACK *as he listens to* LIONEL.)

LIONEL. Don't you worry, Bernard. I can speak for Ken Frazer. There's only one reason he was late at my wedding. That's 'cause he had to take their Boris to the hospital. Their Boris had been sucking a penny and he swallowed it.

JACK. He's not getting Ken Frazer, is he?

BERNARD (*showing some slight signs of alarm*). Why?

JACK. You what! Haven't I ever told you this? When our foreman's daughter got married and they wanted a photographer. So Muggins here chimes in and puts him on to Ken Frazer. There was hell to pay.

ALICE (*complacently*). He didn't turn up.

    (CHRISTINE *crosses to join the group.*)

JACK. He turned up—I wish he hadn't. He had them stood there for three-quarters of an hour. And do you know how many pictures came out in the finish? One. Rotten lousy one. And that's all they've got. They've got one picture of the two of them getting into a car like this. (*He assumes a crouching position.*) Our foreman blames it all on to me.

    (*The door opens and* STAN DYSON *enters and stands hesitantly in the doorway trying to catch* IRENE'S *attention.*)

BERNARD. Well, it must have been one of his off-days, 'cause I've seen some of his pictures and I think they're good.

CHRISTINE. What's up?

BERNARD. Ken Frazer. Jack's saying he doesn't think much of him.

JACK. Think much of him! He couldn't photograph the back of our house.

CHRISTINE. Aw, nobody's any good to hear you talk.

    (ALICE *drops her voice and indicates* STAN *who is still endeavouring to catch* IRENE'S *eye from the door.*)

ALICE. I say! Who's that? Does anybody know him?

CHRISTINE. No. I don't know him.

    (*They all turn and look inquiringly at* STAN *as* EDGAR *crosses to speak to* STAN.)

EDGAR. Are you looking for somebody?

STAN (*staring pointedly at* IRENE). Irene Howes. Is she here?

EDGAR. Well, she's here but we're a bit tied up at the present moment.

STAN. Well, can I have a word with her?

EDGAR (*turns and calls across the room to* LILIAN). Lilian! There's someone asking for your Irene.

LILIAN. Oh, it's only Stan. He can come in.

STAN (*marching across to* IRENE). I've been waiting at the top of your street for the past half an hour.

IRENE. Well, I couldn't get away. I told you I couldn't come out tonight.

STAN. I told you to meet me at the top of your street.

IRENE. Well, I couldn't come, Stan. Don't say I didn't tell you. I told you our Christine was getting married. I've had to help.

STAN. You knew I was waiting, didn't you? I've been waiting there for half an hour.

LILIAN (*turning to* RHODA *and speaking indulgently*). This is how they are. They're like this all the time.

STAN (*mildly indignant*). It's all right for you, I've been stuck out in the freezing cold.

LILIAN. Get away with you; it won't hurt you.

STAN (*dogmatically to* IRENE). Well, why didn't you come then?

IRENE. I couldn't. I've been helping my Auntie Rhoda.

STAN (*partly placated but reluctant to give up the argument*). Well, I thought you were supposed to be meeting me at the top of your street.

ARTHUR (*still carrying his empty pint glass, has wandered over to join* STAN *and* IRENE. ARTHUR *stands in front of* STAN *looking at him keenly*). Now then, young man.

STAN (*puzzled*). How do?

ARTHUR. You don't know me, do you?

STAN. No, I can't say I do.

ARTHUR. No, you don't. But I know you. I've known you since you were the size of sixpennorth of copper. I know your father. You just tell him when you get home. Tonight. Tell him you've seen Mr. Broadbent. He'll know. Ask him who put him on the last tram on St. Leger Day. He'll know who you mean.

STAN. I'll tell him. Mr. Broadbent.

ARTHUR. You still don't remember me, do you?

STAN. I can't place you.

ARTHUR. By bloody hell! Many and many a time I've given you threepence for yourself.

> (ARTHUR *turns and announces* STAN's *identity to* RHODA *and to the room in general.*)

It's Alf Dyson's lad, Rhoda. You know Alf Dyson. Him who always got you them rabbits.

RHODA. I knew I'd seen him.

LILIAN (*to* STAN). Well, you never told me you knew Arthur.

STAN. Well, I didn't know I knew him. How did I know I knew him?

LILIAN. You'll have to remember people's faces from now on. 'Cause there's a lot of us in the family.

ARTHUR (*genially*). Well, he'll know me next time he sees me.

(IRENE *crosses almost shyly and whispers to* LILIAN.)

LILIAN (*in reply*). What? Oh, I don't know, it's nothing to do with me. You'll have to ask your Auntie Rhoda about that.

IRENE. Well, you ask her.

LILIAN (*impatiently*). Oooh, you're like a kid sometimes. You're like I-don't-know-what! (*To* RHODA.) She wants to know if Stan can come to the wedding?

RHODA (*rather embarrassed*). Well, I don't know. We don't object to anybody coming—who wants to. But I wish he'd spoke up a bit earlier. What do you think, Edgar?

EDGAR. Well, I mean, it's a family do, like, isn't it? I mean, you please yourself. It's for our Christine to say—not me.

CHRISTINE. I don't mind. He can come if he wants. The more the merrier.

RHODA. He'll have to make his own way. There's been transport difficulties.

IRENE. Can he come then?

STAN (*edgily embarrassed at this discussion about himself and turning on* IRENE). Shur-rup!

RHODA. He can come if he wants to. Nobody's stopping him. He'll have to take us as he finds us. (*She dismisses the subject.*) Anyway, if he's coming he can give us a hand now. Get finished off. There's these glasses to get sorted out yet.

CHRISTINE. I'll see to them, Mam.

(CHRISTINE *crosses to the case of glasses which* LIONEL *and* MARGO *carried in. As* CHRISTINE *attempts to lift it she is joined by* EDNA, *who helps her to carry it to a table.*

CHRISTINE *and* EDNA *are joined by* MARGO *and they, during the following dialogue, unpack the glasses and polish them. The other occupants of the room busy themselves in a final tidying-up sortie.*)

MARGO (*to* CHRISTINE). Anyway, love, I hope you have better weather than we did, tomorrow.

CHRISTINE. Why—did you have rain, at your wedding?

EDNA. Rain? It pelted down, all day. Never stopped. And I caught a cold, and I could not shake it off. I was in bed with pleurisy by the time I'd finished.

MARGO. And our Harold was eating an orange in his page-boy suit before we set off and he had all juice, all down here. It had to stay— we hadn't time.

EDNA. Car didn't turn up—we had to go down to that telephone box on Top Moor Road and phone up for a taxi. Speedway Cabs. Flowers were late.

MARGO. Cake gets lost.

EDNA. Our Dennis loses his wallet.

MARGO. Not enough sherry.

EDNA. It was a day and a half. I'll tell you.

MARGO. We can laugh now, but we weren't laughing then.

CHRISTINE. Well, you always get something goes wrong, don't you?

MARGO. Your weather's the biggest gamble.

CHRISTINE. They say it's going to be fine tomorrow.

EDNA. They say a lot of things, love.

RHODA (*approaching the group*). Now then, are we going to have enough glasses to go round?

MARGO. Well, not counting the kiddies. They'll be having their beakers.

RHODA. Orange juice! I've just remembered. Christine, will you remind me when we get home? And I'll put a bottle out. Your dad can bring it down in the morning.

(STAN *and* IRENE *cross and join the group.*)

IRENE. Hello, Mam. Does my Auntie Rhoda want me any more? 'Cause Stan's got to get off. 'Cause he'll have to get up early in the morning. 'Cause he'll have to go into town and get a shirt, if he's coming to the wedding.

(LILIAN *folds her arms and looks at* IRENE *and* STAN *sternly.*)

LILIAN (*to* RHODA). And that's somebody else who's going to be putting us all out very shortly.

RHODA. Who—your Irene?

LILIAN. Yes—she's reckoning on getting married, now. (*Sharply to* IRENE.) Aren't you? Eh? Aren't you?

IRENE. We're only getting engaged, that's all.

RHODA. Wonders never cease. When you getting engaged, love?

IRENE. On Boxing Day.

CHRISTINE. When are you getting married?

IRENE. We're thinking about August Bank Holiday, aren't we, Stan?

STAN. All being well.

IRENE. I know what wedding dress I'm having, I don't care what any-body says. It's waltz length, puff sleeves, plunging neckline.

LILIAN. Never mind your plunging neckline, you want to get saved up first.

IRENE. It's all right, is this dress. It was in last week's *Debbie*. It's good, is *Debbie*. They're giving out a *King of the Gipsies Dream Book* next week.

STAN (*shifting impatiently from one foot to the other*). Anyway. What we
    doing, Irene?
IRENE (*to* LILIAN). Well, can we go, Mam? 'Cos he's got to get up and
    get his shirt.
STAN (*embarrassed*). Shur-rup about blooming shirt! Anyone'd think I
    hadn't got a shirt.
IRENE. Well, you haven't got one fit to wear, have you?
STAN. 'Course I have. I've got that cream one, haven't I? In the wash.
IRENE. Oh, well you haven't got one clean then.
STAN. Are you coming, or aren't you?
RHODA. Oh, go on, Irene, get off if you're going. There's enough
    people standing about doing nothing.
    (IRENE *turns to* CHRISTINE *and rather gabbles her parting words.*)
IRENE. Anyway, I'll see you tomorrow, love, and I hope all goes well
    and I hope you'll be able to give me a few tips when it's my turn.
    (STAN, *who has crossed to the door, turns impatiently.*)
STAN. Co-ome on!
    (IRENE *crosses to the door.*)
LILIAN (*calling after her*). And think on. What time you've got to be in.
IRENE. All right, Mam. Do you want any chips bringing in?
LILIAN. Go on. Chip off.
    (IRENE *follows* STAN *through the door.* RHODA *surveys the room.
    We follow her glance and note that out of the previous chaos some sort of
    order has arisen. The room is now as tidy as it will ever be.*)
RHODA. Well, I think we can all be putting our coats on. There's
    nothing else we can do tonight.
LILIAN. Well, I shall have to be getting off for one, else that silly cat'll
    be standing in the street waiting for me again. She hasn't the gump-
    tion to look under the mat for the key, same as everybody else.
RHODA. Anyway, he looks a nice enough lad for her.
LILIAN. He's all right when he's working.
    (LILIAN *turns to* CHRISTINE *and formally and rather awkwardly
    shakes hands with her.*)
Well, I hope it keeps fine for you, love. And speak up in church.
Let's hear you.
CHRISTINE. Good night, Auntie Lilian. Thank you for coming.
    (LILIAN *walks to the door and looks round at the room.*)
LILIAN. Well, it looks all right. What's wrong with it? Good night,
    all.
JACK. Good night, love.
RHODA. Good night, Lilian. Thank you.
    (LILIAN *goes out.* MARGO *looks around. She is in a reminiscent
    mood about her own wedding and is about to settle down for a chat.*)

MARGO. I'll say this much, it looks a lot better laid out than we had ours—and we had the Labour Hall. And that's a much bigger hall. What do you say, Lionel?

LIONEL (*clearing his throat*). Very nice. Very nice indeed. They've done well.

MARGO. It's what I always say—if you want a job doing, do it yourself. 'Cause it's no good relying on other people. You get these catering firms in, and you don't know, they might have five weddings in one day. So, of course, they don't bother about you. They start at the last minute and you don't know, till you get there, what they've made of it.

(EDGAR *crosses, looking at his watch.*)

EDGAR. Well, just before we start the mothers' meeting—you know we've got to be out of here by nine o'clock, don't you? We've only booked for two hours tonight, you know. And I know him—he'll charge us.

JACK. I know where I'm going. I'm going for a crafty pint, that's where I'm going! Are you coming down, Dad?

EDGAR. Are you having one downstairs?

JACK. Am I hellers like. I'm going to the Rose. What you doing, then?

EDGAR. I'm coming. I've done my whack. What you doing, Arthur? Are you coming?

ARTHUR. I'm not coming to the Rose. You don't see me in there. I shall have one downstairs.

EDGAR. Could you do with a drink, Rhoda?

RHODA. It's a cup of tea I'm gagging for. Go on—and don't be late in the pair of you. There's a stack of work to do at home yet.

EDGAR (*looking round the room with some satisfaction*). Well—we've not done so bad. We've not done so bad at all. It looks all right, that grease-proof paper—once you get it down.

(JACK *and* EDGAR *cross to the door.*)

JACK. Have you got any money, Mam? Sling us your purse.

RHODA (*tolerantly*). Go on. Don't have so much off.

EDGAR. I'll see you tomorrow, Arthur.

ARTHUR. Yes—some time.

EDGAR. Good night, then. Good night, all. Good night, Mrs. Fuller.

(JACK *and* EDGAR *go out.* LIONEL *calls across the room to* ALICE.)

LIONEL. Are you coming then, Mother?

ALICE (*glancing balefully in* MARGO'S *direction*). Well, you're going up with her, aren't you?

LIONEL. We can all go together—what's the matter with you?

MARGO. It's all right by me. She can suit herself.

(ALICE, *by speaking to* MARGO, *is offering the olive branch, but feels obliged to keep up her critical tone.*)

ALICE (*to* MARGO). Well, I hope you get something on your feet to-morrow. I don't want you slopping into church like that.

MARGO. Oh, Christine doesn't care what I wear so long as I'm there—do you, Christine?

CHRISTINE. I expect I'll have more to worry about.

LIONEL. We'll get off, then. There's a seventeen-A in five minutes. Are you ready, both of you?

(ALICE, LIONEL *and* MARGO *are moving to the door.* ALICE, *who has done no more than desultorily lift up a duster, looks round approvingly and speaks in a self-congratulatory manner to* RHODA.)

ALICE. It just shows what you can do when you all pitch in, doesn't it?

RHODA (*drily*). Yes—we've done a lot of work—some of us.

ALICE. It's going to look very nice.

LIONEL. Good night, then. Thanks for having us.

CHRISTINE. Good night. Thank you.

(LIONEL, MARGO *and* ALICE *troop out.* RHODA, *who has been packing her things together in a plastic hold-all, pulls the zip with an air of finality.*)

RHODA. Well, I'm doing no more tonight. Not down here, anyway. Would you like to come up for a cup of tea, Mrs. Fuller, before you go?

EDNA. I shall have to have something before I face that hill. Because it knocks it out of me, does Coalhill Rise.

RHODA (*turning to* CHRISTINE). Don't forget to turn the light off. And cover that cake up before you go.

CHRISTINE. Do you think it looks all right, Mam?

(RHODA *looks round tenderly. The room has now a pathetic grandeur of its own.*)

RHODA. They can say what they like—about Whittaker's or anybody else. I don't think it could look any better.

EDNA (*ungrudgingly*). It'll do. (*To* BERNARD.) And you won't be long, will you—because I don't want to be stopping up all night.

BERNARD. I'll be home before you are.

RHODA. It's no use offering you a cup of tea, Arthur?

ARTHUR. It bloody isn't. I'm off downstairs—that's as far as I'm going.

(RHODA *and* EDNA *cross to the door.* RHODA *takes a last look round.*)

RHODA. I wonder if they're sending any doilies?

(RHODA *and* EDNA *go out. There is a moment's pause while* ARTHUR *looks from* BERNARD *to* CHRISTINE *and self-consciously realizes that besides them he is the last to leave.*)

ARTHUR. Well, I'll love you and leave you then.

CHRISTINE. Good night, Uncle Arthur.

(ARTHUR *pauses self-consciously for a moment and then importantly and ponderously sets down his pint glass for the first time and takes out his wallet. He selects a pound note and moves across to* CHRISTINE.)

ARTHUR. Where do you say you're going then—Scarborough?

CHRISTINE. Yes—just for a few days.

ARTHUR. Well, listen here. When you get there, go into that little café with the corrugated iron roof. That one on the cliff top and just say Arthur Broadbent sent you. See what they say.

CHRISTINE. All right—we will.

ARTHUR. And if I don't get the chance to speak to you tomorrow— here's a pound note to take with you.

(*He thrusts the pound note gruffly at her.* CHRISTINE *takes it.*)

CHRISTINE. Thank you.

ARTHUR. Right. And think on.

(*He picks up his glass and stumps out of the room.* CHRISTINE *holding the pound note, smiles at* BERNARD. *They are suddenly very close.* CHRISTINE *looks round the room.*)

CHRISTINE. What do you think, Bernard?

BERNARD (*following her glance round the room*). Yes, love. It's very nice.

(CHRISTINE *looks critically at one of the tables. Then she walks over and moves a plate a fraction of an inch.*)

CHRISTINE. I don't think we'd have been any better off with Whit-taker's.

BERNARD. I'm sure we wouldn't.

CHRISTINE. We'd better be going.

BERNARD. Yes, love. I'll walk you up.

CHRISTINE. Last time.

BERNARD. Yes, love. Last time.

(*They cross slowly towards the door, and their hands meet. They pause at the door and take a last glance around the room.*)

CHRISTINE. Oo—cake!

(*She hurries across the room and puts a teacloth over the cake. She crosses back to join* BERNARD *at the door. Again they look around the room.*)

BERNARD. Come on, love.

(*He switches off the light. They go out and the door closes softly behind them.*)

THE CURTAIN FALLS.

2. THE FUNERAL

Time: Six months later.

THE MOURNERS

EDGAR LUCAS..	James Cossins
RHODA LUCAS	Gabrielle Hamilton
JACK LUCAS ..	Colin George
LILIAN HOWES	Hilary Hardiman
IRENE HOWES..	Virginia Stride
FRANK BROADBENT	Jeremy Kemp
STAN DYSON ..	Donald Burton
BERNARD FULLER	Michael Williams
CHRISTINE FULLER	Carole Mowlam
EDNA FULLER ..	Thelma Barlow
MAY BECKETT	Colette O'Neil
SERGEANT-MAJOR TOMMY LODGE ..	Robert Lang

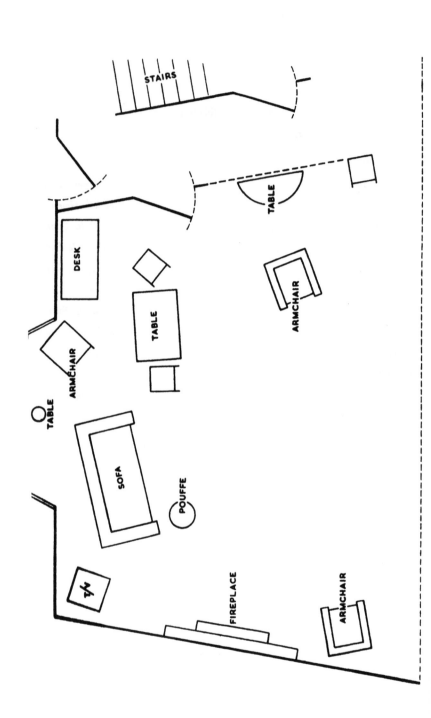

THE FUNERAL

The play is set in the living-room and hall of the Lucas *home—a large terrace-house with about six square feet of garden at the front. The room is furnished with a curious mixture of new and old. There is a fairly new three-piece suite in uncut moquette, an old-fashioned sideboard, a new radiogram, an old dining-room table and chairs and a new television set. There is a new and hideous tiled fireplace above which there hangs a large framed photograph of the late* Arthur Broadbent *in an army corporal's uniform of the First World War. In the corner of the frame is tucked a Flanders poppy. The room is decorated with photographs in a variety of framing styles—rather than with the usual paintings of "crinoline ladies", etc. On top of the television set is a very bad enlargement of the wedding of* Christine Lucas *and* Bernard Fuller. *There is a door leading to the hall, kitchen and front door. There is a bay window looking out on to the privet hedge and street. On the table there are standing, rather self-consciously, two bottles of V.P. port, a bottle of whisky, a bottle of lemonade and an odd collection of various glasses most of which are decorated with transfers of "Bambi" or vintage cars.*

The hall is a dark and gloomy passage—serving only to lead from one room to the next and therefore considered not worthy of that close attention to decorative detail which distinguishes the rest of the house. There is a flight of stairs leading to the bedrooms. One end of the passage leads to the kitchen and the other to the front door. There is a door under the stairs leading to the cellar. There is a cardigan hanging at the foot of a banister and a long row of pegs on which hang a number of macintoshes, jackets, a tartan umbrella and a paper carrier-bag. There is also a bicycle leaning against the wall.

> Irene Howes *is crouched on a minute three-legged stool by the fire and reading a girl's comic. She is eating a bar of chocolate and drinking a glass of lemonade. The record player on the radiogram is blaring a "pop" tune.* Irene *is enjoying the complete contentment of this accumulation of good things—a good fire, good food, good music and good literature. The front door opens and* Jack Lucas *enters and crosses into the living-room.* Irene *rises in some confusion.*

Jack. You're all right, aren't you! You what! Take your shoes off! Put your feet up!

> (Irene *attempts to swallow the mouthful of chocolate.*)

Irene. I wasn't expecting anybody back till quarter to.

Jack. I can see you weren't. Sitting there guzzling. Ramming it down.

> (Irene *crosses and switches off the radiogram.*)

Irene. Where's your mam and dad?

JACK (*removing his overcoat*). Aren't they here yet? They set off before
I did.

(JACK *crosses into the hall. He hangs his overcoat on a peg as* IRENE
follows him into the passage in her usual plaintive manner.)

IRENE. No. There's nobody here. There's only Stan. He's in the cellar.
He's chopping some firewood for you.

JACK (*reacting with alarm*). What with? What's he chopping? He isn't
chopping that box up, is he?

IRENE. I don't know what he's chopping.

JACK. If he's chopping that box up there'll be hell to pay. It's not ours.

IRENE. Well, don't tell me about it—tell him.

JACK (*indignantly*). It's spoken for is that box. Our Frank's had his eye
on it.

IRENE. No—well, we were just sitting there and he says "Well, I might
as well do something as do nothing, so I'll chop them some firewood
up while I'm waiting".

JACK (*very indignantly*). You don't go into other people's houses chopping up what you want. What else has he been doing?

IRENE. He hasn't been doing nothing. We were just sitting there.
Waiting for you all to come back. And he thought "I'll chop them
some firewood".

(JACK *strides along the passage towards the cellar door.* IRENE *calls
after him.*)

He thought he was doing you a favour. He thought you'd
thank him.

(JACK *throws* IRENE *a crushing glance and flings open the cellar door.*
JACK *calls down the stone steps.*)

JACK. Stan! What you doing? What you think you're chopping up?
. . . You what? What for?

(IRENE, *who has been watching* JACK *with growing consternation,
turns as the front door opens.* RHODA *and* EDGAR LUCAS *enter the hall,
leaving the door open behind them.* RHODA *huddles herself with deliberate
exaggeration.*)

RHODA. It's always freezing up there.

EDGAR. They always are—cemeteries. They're always up on hills.
You just notice. Always.

(CHRISTINE *and* BERNARD FULLER *enter and close the door behind
them.* CHRISTINE, BERNARD, EDGAR *and* RHODA *take off their coats
and hang them in the passage as* JACK *moves along towards the group.*
CHRISTINE *is five months' pregnant, and although this is barely physically
evident, it is certainly evident through* CHRISTINE'S *bearing. Falling
automatically into her natural role of motherhood, she walks and sits like
one in an advanced state of pregnancy.*)

JACK. You know what Stan's done, don't you?

    (*A look of mild alarm is shared by* BERNARD *and* EDGAR.)

He's only chopped that box up.

EDGAR (*with resignation*). What did I say he'd do if we let him stop here?

RHODA (*dismissing the subject disparagingly*). Oh, it's only a box when it's there.

    (RHODA, IRENE *and* EDGAR *move into the living-room as* JACK *calls after them.*)

JACK. You try telling our Frank it's only a box! (*To* CHRISTINE.) He'll go bald when he comes in, he will.

    (CHRISTINE, JACK *and* BERNARD *move into the living-room.*)

    (*The six relatives, once in the living-room, are very conscious of their status as mourners and arrange themselves self-consciously on chairs about the room. They all sit perched uncomfortably on the edge of their chairs as if in an alien house. There is a long silence during which* EDGAR *coughs discreetly.*)

RHODA. Well, it seemed to go off very well—to say.

BERNARD. Very nice. Very nice indeed.

IRENE. Were there many there, Auntie Rhoda?

RHODA. Oh, there were ever so many there. They were all there. There was all us, for a start. There was half Cobden Street where he used to live—well, they didn't come for their tea but they were at your graveside. And then, of course, there was your Legion representatives. Six old men, they were grand fellows. They all served with Uncle Arthur.

    (*All the members of the room look dutifully and respectfully at the photograph of* UNCLE ARTHUR *above the fireplace.*)

EDGAR. Who's been drinking lemonade then?

IRENE. I had a glass while we were waiting. You don't mind, do you, Uncle Edgar?

    (EDGAR *rises and shuffles, he attempts to be genial although he has taken offence. He speaks in a higher tone than normally.*)

EDGAR. Well . . . (*He gives a mirthless laugh.*) Well, I mean, you don't go drinking lemonade while there's funerals going on. I mean, you show some respect, as a rule.

JACK. Gerraway! What you been doing down at the Co-op Hall for the last hour! He's had three pork pies, two mugs of tea, ham roll, custard slice (*Inventing wildly.*) sausage roll, chocolate cake, jelly, trifle—

RHODA (*cutting in on her son sharply*). Shut up you! You know what your father means! (*To* IRENE.) You see, Irene, it's just a question of the way things are done. You see, even if you don't attend at the funeral you're supposed just to show that little bit of respect. (*With rising indignation.*) You see, having a cup of tea's one thing—but you don't sit here golloping pop and reading comics when somebody's dead! Damn it all! Let's have a bit of respect!

(IRENE *is too confused to reply and there is again a pause.* EDGAR *slowly bends and picks up a chocolate wrapper from the fireplace. He uncreases the wrapper slowly.*)

EDGAR. She's made herself right at home. She's been eating Munchy-Bars as well.

JACK. I tell you, it's like home from home, is this. There's Irene supping lemonade, there's him chopping firewood. (*To* IRENE.) You want to move in—pair of you. Get your beds round here.

(IRENE *attempts to ingratiate herself back into the company by making a weak joke.*)

IRENE. We might take you up on that, when we get married. We could do with somewhere to live.

RHODA (*half to herself*). Silly cat!

(CHRISTINE *and* BERNARD, *who are sitting together on the edge of the settee, have purposely remained silent during the above as a mark of respect for the deceased. It is their first funeral together since their marriage and they have a sense of occasion.* CHRISTINE *now turns to* BERNARD *and speaks in an attempt to draw the conversation back to a decent level.*)

CHRISTINE. There were some lovely wreaths.

BERNARD. Very nice. Very nice indeed. I like the one that we kindly sent.

RHODA. There wasn't one from Dixon's Boilers, I noticed. You work for a firm for what—thirty-five years was it? And they can't even send a wreath.

EDGAR. Well, they might not have known, you see. He's been left there five years. It's a very big firm. I mean, they've got two thousand people down there, you know.

RHODA. 'Course they knew. They must have known. He'd plenty of mates down there. Well, they reckoned to be his mates anyway. They were his mates on a Friday night. When he was lashing out in the Cricketers.

EDGAR. He didn't go in the Cricketers. He hasn't been in for ages. Not since our Christine got married. (*Looking at* CHRISTINE.) How long's that since?

(CHRISTINE *exchanges a glance with* BERNARD *who clears his throat.*)

BERNARD. August twenty-third. Six months all but two days.

EDGAR. Well, he never went in after that. Terrible row. Terrible.

RHODA. Well, if it wasn't the Cricketers it was somewhere else. They were like vultures. Used to follow him around. Flies round a jam-pot. He was daft with money. Silly daft.

EDGAR. He was very generous. He'd buy anybody a drink, you know.

JACK. I never go in their now, you know. Not since that bother at the wedding.

CHRISTINE. I don't remember any bother with Uncle Arthur.

JACK. Wasn't upstairs, it was downstairs. It was before you got back from the church. It was over May.

RHODA. Don't talk to me about May. I've never known a time when there wasn't bother over that one.

JACK. She wasn't doing anything. She was just waiting in the passage for Uncle Arthur. He'd gone upstairs to the reception room. He'd gone up to put that squeaky cushion on our lass's chair. (BERNARD laughs at the recollection.) He rolls downstairs and there's big-head behind the bar won't serve her. Refuses point blank. He's telling May to get out. He went mad did Arthur.

CHRISTINE. I don't remember.

JACK. I'm telling you you don't. You weren't back from the service. He went mad. I've never seen him like it.

RHODA. He should not have brought her anywhere near that wedding reception. Who is she? She's nobody. Just somebody he picked up in a public house.

JACK. She's all right.

RHODA. How can she be all right? You don't go living with men if you're all right. Not a man of his age. I know what she was after. And he ought to have had more sense than to have took up with her.

EDGAR. Ah, well. He's dead now so . . .

RHODA. And what was she doing at the funeral? She'd no right to be there. She wasn't a relative.

JACK. She wasn't doing any harm.

EDGAR. You'd have thought she'd have put something black on if she was coming.

IRENE (helpfully). She hasn't got anything black, Uncle Edgar. She's only got two coats. She's got that red velour, and she's got that green one with a big thick belt and that scottie dog brooch.

RHODA (turning on IRENE who is still in disgrace). It's nothing to do with you. And what's Stan supposed to be doing?

IRENE. He's chopping firewood.

RHODA. Well, go tell him to stop chopping firewood. He's no business to be chopping firewood.

(IRENE rises and stands smiling uncertainly.)

IRENE. Have I to?

RHODA. 'Course you have! If he wants to chop firewood let him go round to his own house and do it.

(IRENE moves towards the door. JACK calls after her.)

JACK. Watch he doesn't chop you up!

IRENE (*topping this repartee*). He wouldn't do that.

(IRENE *goes out into the hall as the front door opens and* FRANK BROADBENT, LILIAN HOWES *and* EDNA FULLER, *enter.*)

IRENE (*calling back into the room*). There's my mother and my Uncle Frank. (*To* LILIAN.) Hello, Mam! I'm off into the cellar.

(IRENE *moves along the passage and down into the cellar as* FRANK, LILIAN *and* EDNA *enter the living-room.* EDGAR *rises and crosses to the table.*)

RHODA. It's taken you some time.

(*During the following dialogue* FRANK *and* LILIAN *take off their coats.* EDNA *keeps her coat on and sinks into a chair.*)

EDNA. We had to stop twice. I had to get out and walk round. Else I'd have fainted.

BERNARD. Aren't you feeling well, Mother?

EDNA. I'm not feeling well. It's ever since we were in that cemetery. (*Rubbing herself.*) It's all up my back and down my arm.

(LILIAN *hands her coat to* FRANK *who takes it, with his own, and hangs them in the hall.* EDGAR *turns at the table and appeals to all the occupants of the room.*)

EDGAR. Anyway, is there anyone here who thinks there's anything wrong in having a drink?

(*There is a moment's silence.*)

RHODA. I'm not stopping anybody from drinking—if they want to drink.

EDGAR. It's what he'd have wanted.

RHODA. So you say.

(FRANK *re-enters from the hall and stands at the door.*)

JACK. Go on, what's up with you? Get it poured out.

(FRANK *crosses into the room, rubbing his hands expectantly.*)

FRANK. There's nothing wrong with having a drink at a funeral, surely to God?

RHODA. It's how you feel yourself. You have to follow your own beliefs.

JACK (*jocularly*). Well, I believe I'll have a whisky.

(*The tension relaxes and* EDGAR *pours out a number of drinks from a bottle of the V.P. port. As the conversation continues* EDGAR *distributes glasses of port to all.* RHODA *accepts a drink grudgingly.* CHRISTINE *refuses the drink, waving the glass away. The others accept their drinks without verbal acknowledgement.* FRANK *takes up a commanding position in front of the fire and addresses the room.*)

FRANK. Anyway, I'll tell you one thing: if they call that an inclusive funeral service, I'm a blackie.

BERNARD (*self-consciously*). I thought it went very well—to say.

FRANK. You what! You've got a Bentley hearse, your number-one leading car's a Rolls-Royce and your other car's an Austin Princess. You see, there's no conformity. Look at your drivers. One wears gloves and another doesn't wear gloves. Well, you either wear gloves or you don't wear gloves. You don't leave it to the individual.

RHODA. You can say what you like, Frank. I was satisfied. Highly satisfied.

BERNARD (*having latched on to the phrase*). Well, I thought it went very well—to say.

FRANK. To the layman, yes. But, you see, I know Farraways. I know them very well. I've had dealings with them before. They're simply not equipped as an A1 funeral furnishers. You know what he's got, don't you? He's got his hearse. He's got his D.L.W. van for transportation of caskets from the works. He's got his number-one car and that's all he has got. And when he wants another vehicle he has to come, cap-in-hand, to people like me. And then it's "Please can I have your Austin on a mileage basis."

(*By this time* EDGAR *has distributed the port and, having picked up a glass himself, is leaning on the table listening to* FRANK.)

EDGAR. I noticed there was some discrepancy in his fleet.

FRANK. Well, he's not got the capital. He's nothing behind him. I wish I could lay my hands on one good carpenter, that's all. He would have some opposition then. I'd give up the taxi business altogether. 'Cause if I couldn't substantiate myself as a funeral furnisher better than him, I'd want putting away.

RHODA (*sharply*). There was nothing wrong with that funeral. Nothing! There was only one thing wrong with that funeral and that was her.

LILIAN. It's good to tell you you're talking about. I bet she didn't wear a thick green coat, did she?

RHODA (*grimly*). Yes, you know who I mean, love, don't you?

LILIAN (*proud in the knowledge*). May Beckett. I wouldn't put anything past her now.

EDNA. I know that one. I know her of old.

(LILIAN *addresses* RHODA *in a discreet, but loud, whisper.*)

LILIAN. Well, who invited her?

RHODA. She invited herself. She just rolled up. She didn't come in a car. She didn't come in one of our cars. She invited herself.

FRANK. Well, she tried to get in a car, you know. She tried to get in the number-two car going back.

RHODA. Cheeky devil!

FRANK. They wouldn't allow her access. It's the only thing I will say for them.

LILIAN. She tried to get in our car.

FRANK (*impatiently*). Yes, the number-two car!

LILIAN. And we were already crowded, 'cause we gave Mr. and Mrs. Selby a lift back. 'Cause I heard the driver tell her. He said, "I'm sorry, madam, but you don't get in that car." 'Cause, he says, "that car is only licensed to carry five people."

FRANK. Oh, well; he'd tell her that. You say that to save embarrassment. You see, in point of actual fact, he's licensed to carry seven. Even though it's a taxi that he borrows, while-ever it's under his jurisdiction it counts as a hire-car.

LILIAN. And I mean, we weren't ten yards from the grave-side—'cause it's just up against them railings where he's buried. She'd got hold of that car-door handle and she would not let go.

RHODA. I wish I'd have seen her.

LILIAN. Well, that's what I'm saying, love, you'd gone on. You'd left already.

FRANK. In what we call the number-one car. Principal relatives and chief mourners.

RHODA. I just wish I'd been in that other car, that's all. I'd have shown her.

JACK (*still jocular*). Gerraway! You wouldn't have done nothing.

RHODA. You don't know what I can do when my paddy's up. In fact, I've a good mind to go down to that house now and have it out with her.

EDGAR (*uneasily*). Oh, you don't want to upset yourself. Let well alone. She's not a relative—there's no need to set foot in that house. Ever.
> (EDGAR, *in an attempt to restore the congeniality of the occasion, goes round the room with a bottle of port and refills the glasses of* FRANK *and* BERNARD. *The* WOMEN, *who have been sipping their drinks genteelly, are not yet in need of refills and refuse his offer. The conversation continues above this.*)

EDNA. Well, whose house is it? Was it his house or was it her house? I could never fathom it out.

RHODA. It was his house! It wasn't hers.

EDNA. Oh, because I've been thinking it was hers.

LILIAN (*recounting a familiar saga*). Oh, no! He had that house long before he ever met May. Arthur was in that house when all down the street were four and eleven-pence a week, and that's going back. (*Her voice rises hysterically.*) There was no electricity! There was nothing! They had to traipse down to Old Moor every week with their rent books, 'cause they wouldn't come and fetch it! Well, they're sixteen and six now. He charges sixteen and six and they've still got to boil every drop of water, if they ever want a bath.

(EDGAR, *who has completed his tour, has now returned to the table where he is filling his own glass.*)

EDGAR (*glancing up*). They're very nice houses though, Lilian. Solid built.

EDNA. There's no damp. More than I can say for our house, 'cause it runs down our walls. (*Her arms flail about.*) Down the walls, across the ceiling! And then they wonder—why you're badly.

RHODA. They're beautiful houses. Beautiful! She could have had that house lovely for him, but she wouldn't do anything. It was like somebody's back yard in there. I'm not surprised he was out every night. He was better out than in.

BERNARD (*self-consciously referring to the deceased*). He liked a drink— but you never saw him drunk.

(*There is a short, pained and respectful silence from the occupants of the room at the memory of* UNCLE ARTHUR.)

JACK. He must have got through some beer in his time.

RHODA (*returning to her subject*). Anyway, I can't see her keeping that rent up. Not by herself. You see, I don't think that landlord even knows she lives there. You see, it was in his name. I mean, I don't think she's any right to be there.

FRANK. Ah, well, that's your common law. She's what you call your sitting tenant. You see, Arthur was your statutory tenant, but she comes in by common law. What you call usage.

(IRENE *and* STAN, *coming up from the cellar, enter and stand at the living-room door.*)

RHODA. If I were that landlord I'd kick her out into the street.

FRANK. He can't do that. You see, you've still got your Rent Restrictions Act. It's not been superseded. He'd need a court order to get her out of that house. She's a sitting tenant and that's it.

RHODA. I'd sit her. I'd sit her out in the street. (*Turning to* STAN.) And what have you been doing? I don't remember saying I wanted anything chopping up.

STAN. What's up with you?

RHODA. Well, what have you been chopping up while we've been out?

STAN. I haven't been chopping anything up. Only that old packing case and some stuff.

FRANK. What packing case?

RHODA. What stuff?

STAN. Just some stuff. Some old steps.

RHODA (*speaking with dangerous calmness to the company at large*). He's chopped up the step-ladder.

> (*There is a short but pregnant silence at this news, broken by* JACK *who is the only one present capable of rising above the disaster.*)

JACK (*jocularly*). What else have you chopped up, Stan? Go on, you tell 'em!

STAN. What? Nothing. It was only a pair of mucky old steps and an old box.

EDGAR. Well, thank you. Thank you very much. It's only my steps that I do all my painting and whitewashing with, that's all.

IRENE (*defending* STAN). He's swept up down there, anyway.

EDGAR. It's all right sweeping up. I've got that ceiling to do. How does he reckon I'm going to reach up there without steps.

JACK (*turning and catching* BERNARD'S *eye*). Hey, watch me stir it up! (*Loudly to* STAN.) Tell Frank what you've done with his packing case, Stan!

STAN. What?

FRANK (*unbelieving*). He's not chopped that case up.

STAN. What? 'Course I have. It's only an old box.

FRANK. That, my friend, is a Ceylon cedar-wood tea-chest. It's not an old box. Do you know what it's worth?

STAN. What?

FRANK. Tell me! You tell me how much you think it's worth!

STAN (*defensively aggressive*). I don't know. I don't go around pricing boxes.

JACK (*again mixing it*). No, he goes around chopping them up, don't you, Stan?

STAN. Shur-rup!

FRANK. Well, I'll tell you what that box is worth, my friend. Was worth, I suppose I should say. It was worth thirty-five shillings.

RHODA. How much? That's not what you told us when you asked if you could have it.

FRANK. Ah! Ah well, it's not worth thirty-five shillings to you—but it was worth thirty-five shillings to me. You see, I wanted that box for a purpose.

> (JACK *rises and crosses to the table with his empty glass.*)

JACK (*to* FRANK). Yeh, we know what you wanted it for. Put all your profits in. (*Taking up the whisky bottle.*) Do you want one, Stan? (STAN, *in an attempt to evade further publicity, edges away from the door and towards the table.*)

STAN. I wouldn't mind.

> (JACK *fills two glasses from the whisky bottle.*)

JACK. I know what I'm having. I'm on whisky. (*To* IRENE.) Do you want anything, love? Do you want some lemonade?

RHODA. She's had enough lemonade.

(JACK *places the two glasses of whisky on the table and pours a glass of lemonade.*)

JACK. Get away! She's all right. You're drinking, aren't you?

IRENE. Thank you very much.

(STAN *picks up a glass of whisky from the table and holds it up self-consciously.*)

STAN. Anyway—

(EDGAR *glances around the room and speaks in acute embarrassment, holding his own glass in front of his chest ceremoniously.*)

EDGAR. Right! Well, we've all got a drink. (*Accusingly.*) You haven't got a drink, our Christine.

CHRISTINE. I've stopped, Dad.

EDNA. You do right. There's some goes on, drinking and smoking; then they wonder why the baby's anaemic.

EDGAR (*picking up the lemonade bottle and a glass and pouring* CHRISTINE *a drink*). A lemonade won't hurt her, I'm sure.

EDNA. If she's like me it will. Too gassy.

EDGAR (*handing the drink to* CHRISTINE *and speaking to* EDNA). Gerraway! (*He crosses and picks up his own drink, assuming a formal air. The others, realizing what is about to happen begin to look sheepish.*) Right. Well. If I can just have a minute. (*The occupants of the room listen attentively.*) Well, I think this is a painful occasion for us all—but I don't think Arthur would have minded us having a drink . . . (*Floundering.*) So, anyway, all I really want to say—well, I know I haven't got the gift of the gab like Frank—but he had a good life and he were a good bloke and I think everyone here will agree with that. So . . . and I remember he had his good days and he had his bad days but he was a good bloke and that's all I want to say.

RHODA (*attempting to prompt* EDGAR *in a loud whisper*). Now you say your toast!

FRANK (*clears his throat and taking over the proceedings*). All right! Now before you have your toast I would ask you all to rise. Just for one moment. Thank you! If you'd all just stand!

(*At which point the occupants of the room, now suffering excrutiating embarrassment, shuffle to their feet and hold their glasses self-consciously for the toast.* FRANK *waits for complete silence before he continues.*)

Very good. Now in replying to my brother-in-law's apposite remarks, I would just say this. The late Arthur Broadbent was a man loved and respected by whomsoever came into contact with him. Right?

(At which point there is a loud knock on the front door. RHODA, slightly peeved, motions to IRENE to go and answer the door. IRENE tiptoes out of the room elaborately while FRANK, who has paused only momentarily, continues his speech. During the following IRENE crosses the hall, opens the front door and speaks to someone outside. IRENE then closes the door and returns into the room.)

I have made many dealings with him, both as a relative, a friend and business dealings. I have always found him fair and square and am only proud to have been numbered among his many acquaintances. Right. Now this is not a mournful occasion. We'll all carry on—as Arthur would have dearly wished us to carry on—that is to say, each going about his business in his own way. But I would say this: as we go about with the daily round, we will remember each and every day a man that we were pleased and proud to call our friend, I thank you.

(IRENE has, by now, re-entered the room and is patiently standing directly in front of RHODA, who is politely waiting for FRANK to finish. BERNARD, followed by CHRISTINE, then EDNA and LILIAN, gingerly seat themselves under the impression that FRANK has concluded his remarks.)

RHODA. What is it love?

IRENE. There's someone at the door.

RHODA *(impatiently whispering)*. Well, tell them to come in.

(Before RHODA has time to give IRENE more than a glance of exasperation, FRANK, completely unperturbed, continues. During FRANK's following remarks BERNARD, CHRISTINE, EDNA and LILIAN rise guiltily to their feet.)

FRANK. I would now ask you to join with me. In charging your glasses.

(IRENE looks wildly around for her lemonade.)

And proposing a toast. The toast, ladies and gentlemen, is—to the memory of Arthur Broadbent.

(FRANK raises his own glass ostentatiously and, with the exception of IRENE, who has not managed to find her glass, the others follow suit. IRENE takes the opportunity to speak during the silence while the others are drinking.)

IRENE. Only it's May.

(This disclosure causes a stunned silence for some moments. RHODA hands her glass to IRENE and, pulling herself to her full height, marches briskly out of the room as the remaining occupants shuffle, uneasily. RHODA crosses along the hall and opens the front door to its full extent. MAY BECKETT is one of those people whom grief seems to make more cheerful. But it is an awkward moment for both of them. MAY steps into the hall.)

MAY. Hooh! I've had to walk up!

(RHODA *looks at her in some embarrassment.*)
It's steep, is that hill.
RHODA. Yes.
MAY. Only I thought I'd pop up. 'Cause I didn't get the chance of a word with you up there.
RHODA. No.
MAY (*peering around* RHODA *towards the door of the living-room*). And I knew you had people coming in. To pay their respects.
RHODA. Yes. Well, there's only relatives.
MAY. So I thought I'd pop up. To pay my respects.
RHODA (*reluctantly*). You'd better come in for a moment.
(RHODA *turns and moves towards the door of the living-room, followed by* MAY.)
MAY. There were plenty there.
(RHODA *enters the living-room, followed by* MAY. *The occupants of the room are still standing awkwardly. They are embarrassed by* MAY. MAY *addresses the room in general.*)
I was just saying—there were a lot there.
(*The statement receives no encouragement.* MAY *moves further into the room.*)
MAY. It shows you. He was very well respected.
EDGAR. Oh, he was.
FRANK. Very well respected. Well, I mean, he endeared himself, didn't he?
(MAY, *feeling that the ice has been cracked if not broken, crosses to a chair, sits down, looks around and surveys the standing company.*)
MAY. Oh, there were a lot there. Only you weren't all there, were you? (*To* EDGAR *and* RHODA.) Well, you were there. (*To* FRANK.) And you were there. (*To* JACK.) And I saw Jack. (*To* STAN.) But you weren't there. (*To* IRENE.) And I didn't see you, love.
IRENE. No, we didn't go.
MAY. No.
(RHODA *now feels that some explanation is necessary. During the following dialogue the occupants of the room start to sit down—one by one and looking around to see what the others are doing. They seat themselves in the following order;* EDNA, LILIAN, BERNARD *and* CHRISTINE, EDGAR, IRENE *and* STAN.)
RHODA. Well, she's a bit young. I mean, more than young in years.
LILIAN (*defending her young*). Don't go round saying that, Rhoda. That's not why she didn't go. You said you wanted someone to keep the fire in.
RHODA. Yes, well.
LILIAN. She's been to funerals before. She's not too young.

IRENE (*proudly*). I've been to two, haven't I, Mam? I've been to two funerals, one christening and four weddings. No, five.

MAY. When are you getting married, then?

IRENE. I don't know. We can't get a house, can we, Stan?

(STAN *grunts in reply.*)

LILIAN. You won't try, that's your trouble.

JACK (*standing by the table*). Do you want a drink, then, May?

(RHODA *flashes* JACK *a sharp glance of disapproval and unnoticed by* MAY, *soundlessly mouths the words "No, don't give her one". It is too late however, and* MAY *accepts.*)

MAY. Ta, love. I'll have a milk stout if you've got one.

RHODA. We haven't got any stout.

JACK. You can have a whisky or you can have a port. Which do you want?

MAY. I'll have a whisky then. Just a small one.

(JACK *pours out a whisky for* MAY. *By this time the occupants of the room are seated with the exception of* RHODA, FRANK *and* JACK. *There is another brief silence during which* MAY *glances up at the photograph above the fireplace.*)

That's a lovely photo of him. I think you must be the only one that's got one. I haven't got one. Well, I'm saying I haven't got one—I've got that snap we had—both of us—that what that young fellow took. You know him, Jack. (JACK *hands* MAY *her drink.*) Thank you, love. Oooh, you haven't given me all that, have you?

JACK. Get it down you!

MAY (*Her eyes returning to the photograph*). Only, I was always on at him to get one done. But he wouldn't. He made an appointment once. He was going to go down to Clarks's Studios. Well, we set off but we never got there. We finished up in Bridgecaster. We did! We only called in the Market Tavern for one. Well, there's this pal of his there—in the army. Sergeant-major Lodge. Can he drink! So we rolls out of the Tavern and it's three o'clock. Well, we had to put Sergeant-major Lodge on his bus, 'cause he'd have never got on it by himself. And it's just setting off and I'll go to hell if Arthur doesn't say, "Come on, May, we'll go with him!" And that's where we finished up, Bridgecaster. By bloody hell, what a night that was!

EDGAR. He liked his beer, did Arthur.

BERNARD. But you never saw him drunk.

MAY. Who didn't? Who didn't! You don't know the half of it. There's many and many a time I've had to put him to bed myself. Many a time. Frequently.

RHODA (*almost taking offence*). Well, he's gone now—so—

MAY. You see, he could always get home under his own steam.

That's what they used to say. But once in that house it was a different tale altogether. It used to hit him then. He'd have a cup of tea—well, it's the same as spirits, you see. Whatever they drink. Whether it's tea or milk or beer or tea or what. It was the weight on his stomach. And then he was away. Paralysed. Never saw him drunk! You'd laugh!

RHODA (*now taking offence*). I don't think you should talk about people when they're dead.

MAY (*cheerfully*). Ah, well, we don't all think alike, do we?

RHODA (*now on the attack*). And there's another thing, I didn't want to bring it up but—since you're here—I think you might have shown a bit more respect and worn black.

MAY (*unperturbed*). Oh, it's going out is black for funerals.

RHODA. Or something dark. If you had to go.

MAY (*with a fixed grin*). How do you mean, love? If I had to go?

EDGAR (*uneasily, to* RHODA). You don't want to go bringing that up. What's it matter now who was there and who wasn't there? You won't fetch him back.

MAY. Just a minute, Mr. Lucas. (*To* RHODA.) How do you mean, love? If I had to go?

LILIAN (*confidentially, to* MAY). Take no notice. She's a bit upset.

MAY (*the grin still frozen on her face*). Well, we're all a bit upset. But, you see, this lady's said something and I'd just like to know what it is that she means when she says, "If I had to go."

CHRISTINE (*uneasily*). She didn't mean anything. All she meant was that—

MAY (*interrupting with knife-edged pleasantness*). No, just a minute, love. (*Indicating* RHODA.) It's this lady that we're talking to.

RHODA (*now worried*). I don't know what you're getting so hot and bothered about.

MAY (*completely in control of the situation*). I'm not hot and bothered, love. It's not me that's hot and bothered.

RHODA. Well, that's all right then.

(*The tension relaxes as* MAY *picks up her glass and has a drink.* RHODA, *relieved, sits down.* MAY *finishes her drink in silence and, slowly and carefully, replaces her glass under her chair.* MAY, *resuming her glassy smile, leans forward in her chair.*)

MAY. Oh, but it's not all right, love. You see, you've said something now and you haven't explained what you meant. "If I had to go."

RHODA (*now cornered*). Well, I just mean that we weren't expecting to see you there. At the actual funeral. You see, we thought it would be more for relatives.

FRANK (*attempting to help*). I don't think May quite understands, Rhoda.

About the allocations. (*To* MAY.) You see, we had to ascertain the seating arrangements in advance. You see, we had the chief mourners and principal relatives in the leading car and the rank and file relatives in the number-two. All the other representatives, all the odds-and-sods, had to make their way under their own steam. Shankses pony.

(MAY *has completely ignored* FRANK's *detailed explanation but has waited politely for him to finish. She again addresses* RHODA.)

MAY. How do you mean, love? "More for relatives"?

RHODA (*unhappily*). I don't know what you're driving at

MAY. What you said: "The funeral was more for relatives."

RHODA. Well, I thought more for us. All his relatives.

MAY (*quietly*). And don't you think I'm a relative?

RHODA (*with an embarrassed half-laugh*). Well.

MAY (*with great gusto*). 'Cause I've been living with him for eight bloody years and if I'm not a relative now I never will be. (*Surveying the room.*) What are you all looking down your noses at? You all knew. Honest to God, don't say you haven't been pointing me out, all of you, all these years. 'Cause I'm not blind, you know.

EDNA. Don't look at me, missis. I don't go round talking about people.

MAY. Oh, don't you? What did you say to Mrs. Rathbone then? And what did you say to Mrs. Phillips? And what did you say to Mrs. Johnstone? And this is only the last two weeks I'm talking about. Yes, you need look away. There's only one person in this room that hasn't talked about me to people, and that's young Jack there. (*To* CHRISTINE.) You've had a lot to say for yourself, haven't you, love?

BERNARD (*defending his wife*). You're on the wrong tack there, Missis. I've never heard Christine have a bad word for anybody.

MAY. You're very fortunate then, that's all I can say. She knows what she's said about me. Don't you? Yes. You thought it wouldn't come back to me, didn't you?

CHRISTINE (*uncomfortably*). I don't know what you're talking about, Mrs. Beckett.

MAY. Don't you "Mrs. Beckett" me, young lady. Why don't you call me to my face what you call me behind my back?

CHRISTINE. I don't know what you mean.

MAY. Well, what have you gone red for? (*Turning to* IRENE.) Oh, and that reminds me—I've got a bone to pick with somebody else. How do you come to be so well-informed about what I wear in bed of a night-time?

IRENE (*embarrassed at being singled out*). Who? Me?

MAY (*mimicking her*). "Who? Me?" You might well say, "Who? Me?" Who told you that I wear men's pyjamas when I go to bed?

IRENE (*innocently*). Me Mam.

(LILIAN *throws* IRENE *a despairing glance.* MAY *looks directly at* LILIAN *but, with what she considers to be elaborate sarcasm, continues to address her remarks to* IRENE.)

MAY. Yes, well next time you see your mam, you tell her from me to keep her long nose out of other people's affairs.

(LILIAN *draws in her breath as* IRENE, *the sarcasm having gone over her head, replies helpfully.*)

IRENE. That's me Mam there.

LILIAN (*to* IRENE *with annoyance*). She knows, you silly cat! (*To* MAY.) And if you want to say anything to me—get it said. Only say it to me, don't go all round the houses.

MAY. Well, I could say the same thing to you, couldn't I! I mean, it's a pity you didn't come to me with what you've been saying about me and Arthur.

EDGAR (*remembering the solemnity of the occasion and acting as peace-maker.* Yes, well . . . There's a lot of things it's a pity we can't do anything about. We wouldn't be here today if there wasn't.

MAY (*resuming her cheerful expression*). I'm not falling out with anybody, love, far from it. But I just like to get things out in the open. Get it settled. Then we know where we are and how we stand.

(*The tension again relaxes and the occupants of the room ease themselves into more comfortable positions in their seats.* JACK *crosses and takes* MAY's *glass from under her chair in order to give her another drink. As* JACK *moves towards the table with* MAY's *glass he changes the subject.*)

JACK. So—you'll be on your own down there now, then?

MAY. Yes, well, I've been on my own before—I can do it again.

JACK (*pouring* MAY's *drink*). You won't be getting in the Robin Hood on a Saturday dinner time so much?

MAY. Oh, I don't know. They all know me down there. (*As* JACK *hands her the drink.*) You'll get me drunk. It's no use sitting at home moping, is it?

EDGAR. It isn't. It's no good at all. It's no good to anybody isn't that. It doesn't do.

MAY. And, you see, they all know me. They look after me. And there's a lot gets in there from the Market Tavern, well we knew all them. There's Sergeant-major Lodge—he gets in nearly every week. And that little crippled fellow, he gets in. I shall go down.

EDGAR. Best way. Best way, love.

LILIAN. 'Course, I'm old-fashioned. I don't like going in a pub by myself.

EDGAR. Well, we're not all alike, are we? It's what they say: it takes all sorts.

(*The conversation lapses into another respectful silence for some moments.* MAY *looks around for a new topic of conversation. Her eyes alight on* CHRISTINE.)

MAY. How's married life suit you then? The pair of you?

BERNARD (*enthusiastically*). It's all right.

CHRISTINE. It's all right for him, sitting there. He's got it cushy. Won't have boiled eggs. You've got to cut the fat off his bacon. Won't have apples. (*With considerable surprise.*) He won't eat apples. I don't know what to give him.

EDNA. Oh, he was always like that. Ever since he was a little boy. Won't touch this and won't touch that. No wonder he was always poorly. And his arms and legs—they were like little thin rails.

BERNARD. I'm putting weight on now. It must suit me.

CHRISTINE (*without malice*). It might suit you but it doesn't suit me. You ought to see him at tea-time. What a performance. (*Imitating* BERNARD.) "Oo, I'm not having that fish if it's got skin on it. Oo, look, there's a little bit of skin there, that you haven't taken off." Honestly!

BERNARD (*rather proud of his idiosyncracies*). I don't like skin.

CHRISTINE. You'd think it was him that was having the baby, not me.

LILIAN. I used to eat all sort of funny things when I was having Irene. It was all strawberries with me. Coal I had to have. I had to suck a bit of coal.

JACK. 'Course, he'd eat anything.

MAY. Who—Arthur?

JACK. Yeh. (MAY *cackles reminiscently.*) I've been with him some nights —he's had his tea before he comes out—

MAY. He always had a big tea.

JACK. Yeh, well I'm saying, he's had his tea, we get some beer inside us, then he has a pork pie, he has a packet of crisps, he has his nuts and raisins, he has his cheese snacks, he gets through them. What else does he have? Beef sandwich that thick. Couple of sausages. And if that blind fellow comes in selling mussels he'd think nothing of having a couple of packets of them.

(MAY, *who has been listening to this recital with pride, takes up the story.*)

MAY. Always. Fish and chips when he gets home. Plate of bread and butter. And there's many and many a time he's had me out of bed at two o'clock in the morning, doing him some fried bread. Huh! Could he eat.

RHODA. I liked to see him on Sunday dinner-time. All his ports of call he had—for his Yorkshire pudding. He'd call here first, 'cause we were nearest the pub. He'd have his Yorkshire pudding here, then he'd go down to Lilian's, wouldn't he, Lilian?

LILIAN. Yes, he'd come in. He'd say: "I'm starving, Lilian!" And I had to give him his Yorkshire pudding.

MAY. Then he comes home and he has another two platefuls. And that's before he starts his meat and potatoes. Two platefuls, he had! I had to make it in the meat-tin. Yorkshire pudding tins weren't big enough for him. He had to have his meat-tin. (*Softly and with a sudden sadness.*) I'll have that to put away now.

(*Again there is a silence, but this is a silence for* MAY, *and all the occupants of the room look at her as she sits remembering the past. When at last* MAY *speaks again it is with simplicity and great sincerity, and, although her subject-matter is trivial, she adds to it a depth of meaning.*)

MAY. Custard. He really enjoyed custard. Every Wednesday and every Saturday I had to make him a custard. And he'd sit down on the little buffet by the fire and he'd eat it straight out of the bowl. (*She pauses reflectively.*) And it wasn't all boozing and eating with Arthur. He was a fine man. You don't have to tell me about his faults—I knew them—he was a very fine man. (*She pauses again.*) Every Saturday and every Wednesday, for eight years. And he'd finish it up and he'd sit there, hunched up like this. (*She demonstrates.*) And he'd scrape the bowl out and he'd say, "I feel better for that." And I'd say, "You look like Little Jack Horner sitting there." And he'd say, "That's who I am, Little Jack Horner, sat in me corner." And I'd say, "Get away, you great fat pig." (*With great tenderness, and shaking her head.*) He didn't care what I called him.

(*There is another pause. Although* MAY *has spoken with great feeling she is never at any point near to tears.* FRANK *breaks the mood.*)

FRANK. I'll tell you one thing you've forgotten, all of you. Your acknowledgments. In the paper.

RHODA. Oo, yes—we've that to get in. We'll have to get it written down, what we want to say.

EDGAR. Well, what do you put? (*He hazards an impromptu acknowledgment.*) "Mr. and Mrs. E. Lucas—wish to thank . . ." (*Giving up the effort.*) I don't know. What do you put, Lilian?

FRANK. Oh, you have your set formula. It's formulated for you in your newspaper offices. They work to a strict pattern. You can't put in what you want. Name of deceased. Right? Relatives and next of kin? Right? Then you put in who you want to thank—in order of precedence. Perfectly simple.

RHODA. Well, who do we want to thank? There were so many.

FRANK. You don't thank your relatives and personal friends except verbally—on the spot. It's your representatives of various organizations that's your bugbear. Your official tributes. You've got your

Lodge, you've got your Old Comrades Association, and who else have you got?

MAY (*reciting proudly*). There was a wreath from the Pack Horse, there was a wreath from the Market Tavern, there was one from the Paternoster's Arms and there was a beautiful spray from the Bruton Road Working Men's Club. Beautiful.

RHODA. I don't think we have to name all the public houses.

MAY. Oh, yes! Oh, yes!

RHODA (*tolerantly*). No, you see, you don't, love. It's all gone out has that.

FRANK. It's more your official organizations you want to thank. You see, your pubs, they come under personal friends. Don't bother about the details, May. We'll look after all that.

MAY (*folding her arms and assuming her fixed grin*). I'm very sorry, but I want them public houses written down in that advert.

EDGAR. Well, you can't. If you name one you have to name them all, don't you?

MAY. I want them all.

RHODA (*still intolerant*). Well, you can't. So that's that, isn't it?

MAY. How do you mean, love? That's that?

RHODA. Well, it is us that's putting the advert in, isn't it?

MAY. Oh, if that's your attitude I shall just put my own advert in, and bubbles to the lot of you. I shall put: "Mrs. May Beckett wishes to thank the many friends of Mr. Arthur Broadbent who kindly sent floral tributes." And then I shall just put all the names.

(*There is a long and pained silence as the relatives realize the full implications.*)

FRANK. Ah, well, that puts us in a very difficult position.

MAY. Oh, yes?

FRANK. You see, there are a lot of people might not understand. It's a question of your different name.

MAY (*rising in sudden anger*). You can go and flush yourself, you can! (*MAY marches to the door but without any real intention of leaving. She turns at the door, wheels round the room and takes up a commanding position in front of the group. She speaks with a fury which has been mounting for some days.*) If I've not had a bellyful of this family! You bloody middens, you're nothing else. I've taken all I'm going to take, I'm warning you!

FRANK (*attempting to break in*). Now wait just one little minute.

MAY (*in full flow*). I'm taking no more. You can go so far, and you've gone far enough. It's from the minute he dropped dead. You were down at that hospital like a pack of vultures! And it wasn't him you were worried about, you just wanted to make sure I didn't get

him. It's all you were bothered about! So it didn't look as though
his fancy-woman was burying him. You midden-tins, you're
nothing else!

RHODA. Now, don't you come round here talking like that!

EDGAR. Now, you're just working yourself up in into a state, May.

FRANK (*speaking simultaneously with* RHODA *and* EDGAR *and finally overriding them*). Now the whole point is . . . May I speak! May I
speak! Could I just have a little word? (FRANK *has gained his silence.*)
Now then, May, the whole point is—

MAY (*interrupting him*). Don't you talk to me! You can talk till you're
blue in the face!

FRANK (*raising an admonitory finger and again overriding her*). May I!
May I! (*Again gaining his silence.*) Right! Now we can hear ourselves
speak. (FRANK *leans on the end of the mantelpiece and addresses* MAY *in
confidential tones.*) Now the whole point is this, May. You see, when
you have an official function there are certain rules that have to be
adhered to. You see, it's the society that you live in. It's all official
functions—whether it's a funeral or a christening or whatever it is.
There are certain rules that you've got to abide by. We all understand your long association with Arthur—but there's a price you've
got to pay when you come to the official side. You see, you've no
official status.

MAY (*pathetically puzzled*). But I lived with him.

FRANK (*hypocritically*). Yes, and we admire you for it. But you see, you
never got married, did you? You may very well have had your
reasons. You probably did—I don't know—I'm not asking—I
don't want to know. The fact remains—you didn't. So, Arthur's
next of kin automatically reverts to his blood relatives. It's not
us—it's the society we live in. And another thing, the cemetery
authorities would never have stood for it.

RHODA (*kindly*). We never meant that you should stop away. We
just thought you'd much prefer to make your own way there and
your own way back.

FRANK. Under your own steam.

   (*The entire company has been suitably impressed by the case which
   FRANK has stated and is now once again in sympathy with* MAY.)

EDGAR. We didn't want to hurt anybody's feelings. It was just a
question of doing what was best for all concerned.

LILIAN. And I'm as much to blame as anyone, 'cause I thought you'd
want us to do it. I thought you'd expect us to do it.

EDNA. I kept out of it.

JACK. You know I came down to your house, don't you, May? And
you wasn't in?

MAY. I didn't know you'd been down, love.

JACK. 'Cause I'd come down to explain it all beforehand—how we stood.

MAY. I didn't know you'd been down.

JACK. It was in the afternoon. I came straight up as soon as we heard. You'd gone up there.

MAY. It's funny. Nobody told me you'd been.

JACK. Well, didn't that bow-legged woman tell you that lives two doors up?

MAY (*with dignity*). I don't talk to anybody in that street.

FRANK. Anyway, it must be apparent that some effort was made to make contact with you.

MAY. Yes, well that's all past history. It's what we're going to do about that advert that we're talking about now.

EDGAR. We're not going to fall out over that, May.

RHODA (*aghast*). Oh, no, no, no, no.

EDGAR. We'll collect all the names of all the pubs and clubs and whatever-it-is. Get them all printed in the columns and then nobody's got any ticks.

MAY. Suits me. I don't mind whether it goes under my name or under whose name, just so long as everybody's thanked. 'Cause they cost a lot of money, some of them flowers.

BERNARD (*clearing his throat and speaking self-consciously*). They'll have been very well-satisfied, whoever bought them—'cause they gave every satisfaction.

EDGAR (*with relief*). Ah, well, that's settled then. (*Rubbing his hands together and elaborately playing the host.*) Let's have another drink all of us! Go on, Jack you're a better waiter than I am.

(*During the following dialogue* JACK *goes round the room with the whisky in one hand and the port in the other, filling the glasses. The mood has again relaxed and they settle themselves more easily in their chairs. There is another pause before a desultory conversation starts up.*)

EDNA (*to* LILIAN). Mr. Mallandine didn't look well, did he?

LILIAN. Shocking.

EDNA. He's lost some weight.

(*There is a further silence because no one has anything to say. It is* EDNA *again who eventually speaks.*)

There's a lot of new houses going up, up there.

(*A further pause.*)

CHRISTINE (*to* IRENE). Do you still go down to the Astoria, Irene?

IRENE. No. Stan won't go.

CHRISTINE (*to* STAN). Won't you go?

STAN. No, I don't go. (STAN *shuffles uneasily. He feels that the conversational ball is now in his court, but has nothing to do with it. Then, after a pause.*) Anyway, we're saving up. Supposed to be.

CHRISTINE (*to* IRENE). Are you saving up?

IRENE (*shyly*). Yeh. Supposed to be.

BERNARD (*to* STAN). You want to get it spent—while you've chance.

JACK (*to* BERNARD *with a cynical laugh*). Look who's talking. You what! Lend us a quid, Bernard.

BERNARD. I wish I could. I wish I had one to lend.

CHRISTINE (*to* IRENE). Where are you thinking of living when you get married then?

IRENE. Don't know. We're not bothered. Where we can.

LILIAN (*to* CHRISTINE). She's put her name down for the Council. Tried to. But you can't put it down till you get married.

EDGAR (*to* LILIAN). They can build all these offices though. No waiting list for them. Plenty of them going up.

(*The above conversation has taken place spasmodically and between intervals. When* FRANK *speaks, however, he expects the whole room to listen.*)

FRANK. It's your land, you see, Edgar. It's not your labour. There's plenty of that. It's what you call your industrial development as opposed to your housing development. It's all zones.

(*The above statement completely kills all further conversation on that subject and the occupants of the room gaze at* FRANK *in bewilderment.* FRANK, *feeling that a further word of explanation is called for, rounds off his speech.*)

Y'see.

(*This last profound remark from* FRANK *is followed by a polite silence during which we hear a loud knocking at the front door.*)

RHODA. Somebody else!

JACK. I'll go.

(JACK *moves out of the room.* JACK *crosses and opens the front door.* SERGEANT-MAJOR TOMMY LODGE *stands outside. He is wearing his best uniform and, although it is not yet outwardly obvious, he has been drinking heavily.* JACK *looks at him inquiringly.*)

TOMMY. I'm sorry to bother you. I'm looking for May Beckett. Do you know her?

JACK (*opening the door fully*). She's here.

TOMMY. Would you tell her Sergeant-major Lodge is here? I'm sorry to bother you.

JACK. Come in for a minute.

(TOMMY *takes off his cap respectfully and places it under his arm.* JACK *leads the way along the hall as* TOMMY *repeats his apology.*)

TOMMY. I'm sorry to bother you.

(JACK *enters the living-room as* TOMMY *waits respectfully in the hall.*)

JACK. There's someone for you, May.

MAY (*surprised*). For me? (*Mouthing the words.*) Who is it?

(TOMMY *peers into the room and* MAY *notices him. She speak with genuine pleasure—drawing out the name.*)

Tommy!

(TOMMY, *having been addressed, seizes this as an excuse to make his entry. He enters the room briskly, speaking his condolences as he approaches* MAY.)

TOMMY (*with heavy-handed sympathy*). I'm very sorry, May. We were all deeply shocked.

(TOMMY *and* MAY *shake hands ceremoniously.*)

MAY. Oh, Tommy! Oh, Tommy!

TOMMY (*shaking his head and lost for further condolence*). Yes ... Yes ... Deeply shocked.

MAY (*to* FRANK). This is Sergeant-major Lodge, that I've been telling you about.

(TOMMY, *without any intention of rudeness, ignores* FRANK *and continues speaking to* MAY.)

TOMMY. No, 'cause I've been down there and a woman said that you'd come up here so, I thought, I'll have a walk up before I go back, just in case.

MAY (*to* RHODA). It's Sergeant-major Lodge. You've heard me talking about him.

TOMMY. So, I've missed him then?

MAY (*with great formality*). Yes, we buried him at two-o'clock this afternoon. At Five Lanes cemetery.

TOMMY (*reverently*). Did it all go off well?

MAY. Very well indeed.

TOMMY. I was deeply shocked. Deeply shocked. He was a good lad. Very good lad. Very, very good lad. Very very good lad.

(*To the keener minds present it is becoming obvious that* TOMMY *has been drinking heavily. Although his speech is not slurred his maudlin repetitiveness is beginning to give him away.*)

EDGAR. You'll have been a big friend of his then?

TOMMY. Oh, he was a big friend. Very big friend. Well, I've been friendly with him as long as I can remember. I'm only sorry I missed him.

MAY (*who has been giving him a long and studied look*). By, you've had a few, Tommy.

TOMMY. I have had a few, 'cause it was a shock. I set off early. I set off very early indeed. (*Considering the weight of his own remarks.*) Oh, yes! I was dressed and booked out for eleven o'clock without question. Oh-ten-forty-nine-hours. It's in the book! What can't speak can't lie. I just had the one and I was at the bus stop and on that bus for twenty-past. Quarter-past bus gets here quarter past the other hour—so I'd have been at that funeral before anybody. (*Considering the point.*) Oh, yes! Only I'm sitting on the back of that bus and it's jolting about—and it's jolting me—and I'd got that one inside me. Well, I knew I'd never sit it out to the terminus.

(*During* TOMMY'S *speech* JACK *is pouring him a drink.*)

So, I thought, "Well, I'm sorry, Arthur lad, but my need is greater." And I knew he wouldn't mind. So—the top and bottom of it is that I had to debus at the Thorpe Arms and use their abulutions. Well, there was no further transportation.

MAY (*tolerantly*). So you finished up in the Thorpe Arms did you?

TOMMY. Oh, no! Oh, no! I just had the one there while I was waiting for the quarter-to. (*At this point* JACK *hands* TOMMY *the drink.* TOMMY *turns to* JACK *and gives him his full attention.*) Thank you very much indeed. I don't know your name but thank you. And may you always encounter friendship wherever you go and never want for anything.

JACK (*embarrassed by this fervency*). Cheers.

(TOMMY, *having stated his usual civilities, dismisses* JACK *and turns back to* MAY.)

TOMMY. 'Course, I gets on the quarter-to bus and who should be sitting on the back seat but Captain Yates. Well, he insists on buying me one in the Market Tavern. (*He pauses for a moment, lost in admiration.*) 'Cause he's a gentleman, is Captain Yates. And I'm only sorry, May, that you weren't there to see him.

MAY. I don't know him, do I?

TOMMY. No, but you've heard me speak about him. Captain Yates. M.T. Officer. I.C. Transport.

MAY (*basking in the reflected glory*). Oh, yes, I've heard you talk about him.

TOMMY. Well, listen—listen. Listen to what I'm telling you. We were standing at the bar and we got to talking. Well, of course, I told him about your Arthur and where I was going. And I was saying to Captain Yates—you know, just chatting—that he'd have liked Arthur. 'Cause he would. And Arthur would have liked him.

MAY (*in intense tones*). He got on with everybody, Tommy. No matter what class or who they was. Whether they'd got two-pence or ten pounds.

TOMMY (*eager to continue*). . . . Pounds, yes. Anyway, May, what I

did was I took the great liberty of asking Captain Yates if he'd come
to the funeral with me.

RHODA. He'd have been welcome—more than welcome.

TOMMY (*politely*). Yes, well listen, Missis, what I'm telling you. Well
of course, he didn't want to push himself in—'cause they don't, in
that class. I says "Come on, sir"—'cause I knew he'd be welcome.
But he says—"No, another time, Sergeant-Major." So I says—
Come on, sir, you can take them as you find them—they'll give you
a drink." And he was going to come. He was going to come!

> (*There is a pause while the occupants of the room consider the social
> splendours that would have been within their grasp.*)

EDGAR. He'd have had to take us as he found us.

FRANK. It's a pity he didn't come. 'Cause I'd have had a great deal in
common—if you say he's the M.T. Officer. M.T.—Motor Trans-
port, that's all it means. I.C. Transport—in Charge of Transport.
Well that's what I am, only I don't carry the Queen's Commission.
(*With sudden bitterness at this usurping of his own limelight.*) What is he?
He's nothing. He's nothing but a glorified bloody taxi driver.

RHODA (*sharply*). You don't talk like that. We'd have been very glad
to have had him. You don't know what he is.

TOMMY (*formally*). Captain Yates is one of the finest officers in the
history of the British Army. And I don't care what regiment you go
to. (*Ticking off the exploits of* CAPTAIN YATES *on his fingers.*) He's
been all through France, he's been all through Italy, and I'm going to
tell you something now, he has turned down the opportunity of
being seconded to N.A.T.O., attached—just so he could stay with
his own lads. 'Cause they'd do anything for him.

LILIAN. And was he going to come?

TOMMY. 'Course he was going to come! Only he had the great mis-
fortune to fall down the lavatory steps of the Market Tavern. And I
had to leave him there.

EDNA. Oh dear me! He's not hurt is he?

TOMMY. Well, he's not hurt—no. It shook him. No, he's not hurt
but he picks himself up and, of course, he's fallen in this disinfectant.
I had to leave him there.

> (*The class image which the company has built up of* CAPTAIN YATES
> *is in no way destroyed by the above statement.*)

JACK (*helpfully*). They're too steep, them steps. I've gone down them
myself before now.

TOMMY. Anyway, he sends all his best apologies. And he's only too
sorry not to be here.

MAY. Well, if he gets on with you, Tommy, he'd have got on with

Arthur. (*To the company at large.*) 'Cause they were big pals these two. They were a right pair—when they got going.

EDNA (*who has been hugging a secret to herself*). We know that! You don't have to tell me that, love! (*To* TOMMY.) You don't remember meeting me, do you? (TOMMY *examines* EDNA *quizically.*) It's all right looking. You *won't* remember me, the state you were in.

TOMMY. Why? Had I had a few?

EDNA. You'd had more than a few. You owe me for a butter-dish still, and you won't remember that either. (*To the company.*) There was Arthur, there was our Geoffrey and there was this gentleman. Our Geoffrey had met them both at the Territorials. And they rolled into our house—midnight—with this bottle of green stuff that they'd won. I don't know what it was.

TOMMY (*remembering*). Green Chartreuse! We won it in a raffle!

EDNA. They sat in our house, supping it and doing conjuring tricks. They were sat round, there was Arthur doing his conjuring and then three o'clock in the morning, this gentleman says to me, "Are you hungry? 'Cause", he says, "if you are I'll make you a Lemon Souffle!"

TOMMY (*proudly*). She's right. 'Cause I am a cook. It's not my trade now but I've passed out as one. I did a six-weeks course at Tewkesbury.

EDNA. It was my butter-dish that passed out. And four eggs.

MAY (*who has been laughing to herself during the above*). Arthur's talked about that night many and many a time. He believed in having a good time.

BERNARD (*self-consciously*). He liked a night out. But he never became objectionable.

JACK. I've had some good nights with him.

EDNA. He'd give you the shirt off his back.

IRENE. He was always giving me five shillings, wasn't he, Mam?

LILIAN. He was always good to you, love.

FRANK. He was a very generous man.

(*An almost sentimental atmosphere has grown out of this list of tributes. There is a respectful silence before* MAY *speaks, loudly but as if to herself.*)

MAY. I've seen him come in at night and empty his pockets and he'd say, "Here you are, May, here's a pound note for yourself, it's what I owe you." 'Cause he once borrowed a pound years and years ago when I first met him—and he's given me it back I don't know how many times. Well, he was good enough for me. 'Cause I'm nothing. But he took up with me and he'd take me anywhere. He was never ashamed to be seen with me. And there aren't many women who can say that, I don't care who they are. I don't care if they're the Queen of England. I mean, people look down at me, 'cause he didn't marry me. Well, he wouldn't marry me—I make no secret of it. It's the only thing he wouldn't do. He said, "I've had one basinful and I'm not having another." But, you see, he'd take me out four and five times a week, I didn't stop at home. There's not many *wives* can say that. I've had a very full life since he came into it. I've seen him drunk and I've seen him sober. He's seen me drunk and he's seen me sober. I'm not saying we haven't had rows. He's hit me, he's knocked me about the house. There's still a big stain on our wall where a bowl of custard got thrown at it. (*Fervently and with the deepest sincerity.*) But, oh, he was a lad! Oh, he was a lad!

(*This speech from* MAY *has affected everyone in the room. There is now a new respect for* MAY. TOMMY *has been staring at the photograph of* ARTHUR *above the fireplace during the latter half of* MAY'S *speech. There is a silence before he speaks.*)

TOMMY. He had a moustache in them days, then?

RHODA (*following* TOMMY'S *glance*). Well, they all did in them days, didn't they?

MAY. He was always saying he'd grow one again. But he never did. (*For the first time she very nearly breaks down.*) It'll be funny; being on my own again.

(RHODA, *on a sudden impulse, takes down the photograph from above the fireplace.*)

RHODA. I think you'd better have this, love.

(RHODA *hands the photograph to* MAY *who rises to accept it.* MAY *takes the photograph in both hands and feels its weight.*)

MAY. It's a lovely frame.

(*Both women have been dangerously near to showing their emotions.* RHODA *is quick to cover up.*)

RHODA. Only we're going to decorate this room. And we'd have to take it down anyway. 'Cause it won't go with the wallpaper.

EDGAR (*looking meaningly at* STAN). I don't know what we're going to decorate with. No step-ladder.

(TOMMY *finishes his drink and places his glass on the table, with finality.*)

TOMMY. Anyway, I won't have another. 'Cause I've got some arrangements to keep.

JACK. You're not going, are you?

TOMMY. I've got to. More's the pity.

MAY. It's time I was making a move as well, Tommy. I'll walk down with you if you're walking down.

TOMMY. Well, I am hoping to bump into Captain Yates. He said he
   might be in the Market Tavern—later on.
MAY (*wistfully*). I wish I'd met him. He sounds a nice fellow. (*To*
   IRENE.) I'll tell you what you want to do, love. You want to get
   your name put down for number twelve, Cobden Street. 'Cause I
   can't see myself stopping there much longer.
IRENE (*to* STAN). Oh, Stan, do you think we could?
MAY. 'Course you can. You get down there—Lee and Jacobs, estate
   agents. And you tell them Mr. Broadbent has passed on. It was in
   his name and they won't want me there, I know that.
LILIAN (*to* STAN). You want to get down first thing tomorrow morn-
   ing.
         (STAN *is terrified at the idea of confronting officialdom.*)
STAN. I'm not going down! (*To* IRENE.) You go.
IRENE. I'll go. I'm not frightened.
LILIAN (*to* IRENE). Well, what do you say?
IRENE (*mumbling to* MAY). Thank-you-very-much-Mrs. Beckett.
STAN (*to* MAY). Wait a minute!
         (STAN *slips out of the room, down the hall and into the cellar.*)
EDGAR. Where's he going now?
MAY (*to* IRENE). They're nice houses. Two bedrooms, scullery, living-
   room and a lovely dry cellar. It just wants a good sweep out, that's
   all.
IRENE (*again mumbling*). Thank-you-very-much-indeed.
TOMMY (*who has been lost in his own thoughts*). I've been studying, May.
   I don't know why you don't come down with me. To the Market
   Tavern. You could have one or two and catch a bus up back.
MAY (*again wistfully*). I'd love to, Tommy. Any other day.
EDGAR. Go on. He wouldn't mind. He'd want you to.
JACK. He wouldn't want you to be miserable, May.
TOMMY. And I'd like you to shake Captain Yates's hand.
         (MAY *and* TOMMY *move together towards the door.*)
MAY. All right then. Only I won't stop. I'll just have the one. 'Cause
   I don't want to go back to that house by myself.
         (STAN, *who has now come up from the cellar carrying a bucket of
   firewood, enters the living-room.*)
STAN (*to* RHODA). Can I give her this?
RHODA (*puzzled*). Can you give her what?
STAN. My firewood.
EDGAR (*genially exasperated*). Well, I'll go to bloody hell. It's only my
   whitewash bucket he's given away now. (*To* MAY, *still genially.*) He
   comes in here, he chops up my step-ladder (*Indicating* FRANK.) he
   chops up his box, and now he's giving my whitewash bucket away.

I'll get no decorating done this year, I can see that. (*To* STAN.) Go on, lad, give her it.

(STAN, *with very little grace, hands* MAY *the bucket of firewood.* MAY *tucks the photograph under one arm in order to take it.*)

STAN. Here you are, then.

MAY. Thank you, love.

TOMMY (*impatiently*). We'll have to go if we're going, May.

MAY. I'm coming.

RHODA. And don't stop away so long, next time. Don't leave it another eight years before we see you.

MAY. No, all right, love.

(TOMMY, *his hand on the door, makes a formal and fervent farewell.*)

TOMMY. Well, I'll just say that I'm very glad to have met you all and I hope we all meet again under happier circumstances. Good night then.

(FRANK *acts as spokesman for the company.*)

FRANK. Good night to you. Same to you.

(TOMMY *moves out of the room and up the hall.* MAY, *the photograph under one arm and the bucket of firewood in her other hand, follows him. They go out through the front door. There is a relaxation in the living-room as the front door slams.*)

EDNA. She's aged. She's put some years on.

RHODA. Well, we all have.

LILIAN (*to* IRENE *and* STAN). Anyway, you two have got your work cut out—if you're going to take that house. There's some scrubbing to be done there.

CHRISTINE (*to* IRENE). When will you get married then?

IRENE. I don't know. When we can.

LILIAN. More expense.

RHODA. It's worth it. It's only once.

STAN (*making a joke*). Well, you hope so, don't you?

(IRENE *moves closer to* STAN *appreciating his sense of humour and attempting to cap it.*)

IRENE. Well, you only get married once. You don't get married twice.

EDGAR. You'll need to get your thinking caps on and make all your arrangements. 'Cause it's a job and a half—getting married. There's your invitations, there's your reception, there's your cars.

FRANK. Your cars are no problem.

CHRISTINE. Who do you want for your reception. Barker's?

EDGAR. They don't want Barker's. (*To* LILIAN.) You want to go to Whittaker's. They do everything.

RHODA (*looking up at the blank space above the fireplace*). That's something he won't be coming to.

CHRISTINE (*following her glance*). He enjoyed weddings, didn't he?

BERNARD (*also looking up*). Oh, he liked weddings.

(*Again there is a respectful silence. This time longer than ever before. During the pause, and one by one, all the occupants of the room, with the exception of* FRANK, *turn their gaze towards the unfaded patch of wall-paper where* ARTHUR's *photograph has been.* FRANK *stands with his back to the fire.*)

LILIAN (*to* CHRISTINE). I thought Barker's did you very well—for the price.

EDGAR. On the cheap. It's all on the cheap with them.

(*The mood has again changed. The company has done its duty to* ARTHUR's *memory. Life goes on.* JACK *crosses and picks up a fresh bottle from the table.*)

RHODA. We know you. You want a banquet when you start, you do.

(JACK *begins to move around the room replenishing glasses.* CHRISTINE *rises and crosses to the radiogram.*)

BERNARD. I say, speak as you find. And we were highly satisfied.

(CHRISTINE *switches on the radiogram. It is the same "pop" record that* IRENE *was playing when the curtain went up.* EDGAR *crosses to the coal bucket by the fireplace.* JACK *continues to pour drinks, but now lavishly.* EDNA *loosens her coat as* FRANK *lights a cheroot importantly.* RHODA *kicks off her shoes. There is a comfortable pause.*)

EDGAR. They want to get to Whittaker's. They do it all.

(*The* CURTAIN *begins to fall.*)

RHODA. I've been to some of Whittaker's do's. You get a scuttering bit of lettuce—a scuttering bit of lettuce, a tomato, and a jelly. And it's all paper plates with them. You don't want paper plates when somebody's getting married.

THE CURTAIN HAS FALLEN.

THE WEDDING

Furniture Plot

O.P. D.S. Folded card table
  Two stacked chairs
  Coat pegs
  Double light switch below door
  Clock over door
  "Best Prices" notice U.S. of door on old gas bracket
  Lodge oak chest above door
Back wall U.R. Three billiard cues in rack
  Billiard score marker above rack.
  Three trestle tables stacked against R.C. wall.
  Roll of Honour C. with beer advertisements on either side
U.L.C. Card table
  Overturned chair U.S. of it
  Carton of empty bottles below it
Shelf L. Two advertisements
Over shelf L. Stag's head
R.C. Chair
P.S., D.S. Settee
  Portrait of Queen on wall
Off L. Fifteen chairs

Property Plot

Small empty Double Diamond bottle by wall U.C.
Three empty beer crates in U.R. corner, billiard table against back wall U.R., balloons and cloakroom tickets on floor C. and near fireplace
Top end of sofa D.L. Empty bottle
On card table L. Beer mats, raffle ticket book, dirty ashtray
  Three small empty bottles, two tankards. Cardboard box with empty bottles to R. of table
On shelf L. Beer mats, two tankards, two small bottles, two ashtrays
On chest U.R. Empty bottle and two tankards
By chair R.C. Empty bottle
Leaning on wall U.C. Dartboard with two darts
Off U.L. Broom head and handle, dustpan and brush, Brasso and three rags, jam jar half filled with water
Off D.R. Two wrapped bottles
  Tea urn filled with newspaper
  Step ladder
  Box with twenty-four tumblers
  Tray with twenty-four knives, forks, desert spoons, tea spoons, twelve fish knives
  Two bunches wrapped flowers, flowers in paper bag, all set in brown bucket bag
  Tankard with two bottles of beer (opened at curtain-up)

Three boxes containing wedding cake, top box with cake knife and satin
ribbon, statues on top and pillars on top of those, white cloth to cover
Enamel bowl with hot water and cloth (to be ready immediately after
Frank's entrance)
Carrier bag with two tea cloths, duster, apron and canvas shoes
Tea chest containing: Five vases, twenty-four cups, twenty-four saucers and
plates
Small box with three rolls of greaseproof paper with paper clip in each,
about four doilies
Larger box with twenty-four (minimum) napkins and doilies, wrapped blue
cup, two boxes drawing pins, four large white streamers and one small,
silver roll and cake wrappers (two), bells, horseshoes, etc.
Stool

Personal Props

EDGAR:	Cigarettes, matches and drawing pins
IRENE:	Handbag with photograph of Stan
LILIAN:	Handbag with cigarettes and matches
BERNARD:	Cigarettes and matches, wallet containing photographs and football coupons
EDNA:	Handbag with head-dress in Polythene bag and inhaler
FRANK:	Gloves, notebook and Whiff
RHODA:	Bag with guest list, two Biros, blank cards and purse
MARGO:	Cigarettes and matches
ARTHUR:	£1 note, 5s. and loose change, wallet, bottle opener, cigarettes and matches
JACK:	Drawing pins and cycle clips
ALICE:	Packet of jelly babies

Furniture Plot

O.P. D.S. Landscape painting
Armchair with antimacassar and cushion
Fireplace: Photo of ARTHUR in 1914 uniform, Flanders poppy in corner
Calendar
Two candlesticks
Two vases
Clock
Three letters behind clock
Fire irons D.S. on hearth
Coal scuttle with coal and shovel U.S. on hearth
U.R. T.V. set. *On top:* cloth, "T.V. Times", wedding photo, *over:* small photo
R.C. Pouffe
O.P. U.S. Settee with two antimacassars, two cushions all disarranged
Wall R. of window: Harvest picture
Window: Lace curtains
Curtains
In bay C. Pedestal table with cloth and china dog
In bay L. Wooden armchair

L. *of window:* Radiogram with record
  Landscape painting
  Standard lamp
On wall L. Flight of three geese
U.L.C. Dining table with cloth
  Two chairs
U.S. *of door:* Chair
D.S. *of door:* Side table with lace cloth and baby photo
  Armchair with antimacassar and cushion
  Chair
  Two carpets
In hall: Lace curtains over stained glass windows
  Hat rack
  Cardigan on banister

PROPERTY PLOT

Beside pouffe R. Opened small bottle of Bitter Lemon, half bar of Crunchie, "Valentine" comic
On settee U.C. Crumpled piece of a comic, chair-backs and cushions crumpled, on floor
On table L.C. Bottles of whisky, port and lemonade, fifteen wine glasses, three tumblers, ashtray
By U.S. *of hearth:* Coal scuttle containing coal
On mantelpiece: Ashtray
Off L. (*in cellar*): Whitewash bucket containing firewood
On small table D.L. Ashtray
  ARTHUR's portrait on wall above fireplace

PERSONAL

EDGAR: Prayer book (check cigarettes)
IRENE: Handbag containing compact with mirror
MAY: Handbag containing cigarettes and matches
FRANK: Notebook
BERNARD: Cigarettes and matches
RHODA: Handbag containing cigarettes and matches
JACK: Yale key

Lightning Source UK Ltd.
Milton Keynes UK
UKHW020956110422
401398UK00006B/414